JULIE BOWERS

A New History of Wales

the norman conquerors

Editors:

RALPH A. GRIFFITHS
Senior Lecturer in History
University College of Swansea

KENNETH O. MORGAN
Fellow and Praelector in Modern History
The Queen's College, Oxford

J. BEVERLEY SMITH
Senior Lecturer in Welsh History
University College of Wales, Aberystwyth

A New History of Wales

the norman conquerors

David Walker

Christopher Davies
Swansea

© David Walker

First published in 1977 by
Christopher Davies (Publishers) Ltd
4/5 Thomas Row
Swansea SA1 1NJ

ISBN 0 7154 0302 8

*Printed in Wales by
Salesbury Press Ltd
Llandybie, Dyfed*

Editors' Foreword

'What is history but a nation's memory?' an eminent scholar once asked. By that test, Welsh people interested in their country's past have been suffering from an enforced loss of memory for far too long. At least until after the second world war, there was a great dearth of books on Welsh history. It seemed almost to be assumed that Wales had ceased to have a history since its conquest by Edward I, that because there was no Welsh political state there could, therefore, be no Welsh history save of the most trivial, parochial kind. Until very recently, Sir John Lloyd's great history of the Welsh people held the field almost alone — and that carried the story only down to 1282.

However, the past twenty years have witnessed a dramatic surge of interest in Welsh history in all its aspects. The importance and relevance of the history of Wales as an academic subject is now firmly established beyond dispute. A stream of important works have dealt with a wide range of historical problems, medieval and modern, ranging from the early Celtic church to the politics of the mid-twentieth century. New Welsh historical journals, some dealing with particular regions or themes, others covering Wales as a whole, have increased and multiplied, to their mutual benefit. At the national university, in other colleges, and in the schools of Wales, Welsh history has flourished as never before. It has become one of the boom subjects of our generation. And yet, all too little of this impressive upsurge of scholarship has penetrated through to the ordinary student, still less the general reader. Far too many of the fruits of Welsh historical learning have been reserved only for the benefit of other scholars, in specialist books, journals or research seminars, with only the occasional television or radio programme to whet the appetite of the layman.

A New History of Wales is designed to remedy this state of affairs fundamentally. It aims to provide a series of compact but comprehensive books which will introduce students in sixth forms, colleges and universities, and of course the general reader as well, to some of the major themes of Welsh history. It will span all aspects of the Welsh past — medieval, modern and contemporary; political, socio-economic and cultural. It will also provide, in convenient and attractive form, illustrative documents to show readers some of the kinds of source material available to the historian of Wales. Each volume will stand in its own right as a self-contained study of an important topic; there will be no attempt to impose an artificial unity on the series in general, other than its concern with Wales. The authors will be entirely free to develop their own approach; they will subscribe to no particular philosophy and will follow no special editorial blueprint. Their only brief is to be readable — and to serve the cause of historical truth as they see it. In this way, the editors hope that Welsh men and women of all ages will find new excitement in reading about their nation's past — and perhaps new incentive to ask questions about their nation's present and future.

Ralph A. Griffiths
Kenneth O. Morgan
J. Beverley Smith

Contents

Illustrations

Acknowledgements

Gratitude is expressed to the following for permission to reproduce plates: the Department of the Environment and John Baker (1); The Phaidon Press (2); The Glamorgan County History Trust (3); The National Monuments Record (4); Philip Barker and James Lawson, and J.K.S. St. Joseph and the Cambridge Aerial Survey (5). Figures 3, 4, & 5 are reproduced respectively with the permission of the Glamorgan County History Trust and its General Editor; MacMillan and Co.; and Philip Barker and James Lawson. The other maps owe much to the pioneering work of William Rees, and were drawn by G. B. Lewis.

Quotations in the text are taken from Ordericus Vitalis, *Ecclesiastical History,* ed. M. Chibnall (Oxford University Press, 1969—); *Brut y Tywysogyon,* ed. T. Jones (2 vols., University of Wales Press, 1952, 1955); and Gerald of Wales, *Itinerary of Wales* and *Description of Wales,* ed. R. C. Hoare (Dent).

Introduction

In 1066 an ambitious duke of Normandy crossed the English channel with an army of Norman followers, reinforced by adventurers drawn from northern France. His invasion coincided with a large-scale attack on northern England from Scandinavia. Under the pressure of these invasions the Old English kingdom reeled, and ultimately collapsed. With the army of the northern earls defeated at the battle of Fulford, King Harold of England met and routed the Scandinavians at Stamford Bridge, and made his kingdom safe from immediate Danish attack. He had then to meet the Normans, who had crossed the channel and established a bridge-head at Hastings while he was dealing with the enemy in the north. At the battle of Senlac (or Hastings), Harold was killed, and William and his men held the field. Two months later, William was crowned king of England. He had to face some five years of danger before the military threat to his hold on England had been checked, a threat never more severe than it was in 1069-70 when he had to meet not only enemies in England but also an army from Denmark. By the end of his reign his kingdom was secure, though he was still much alarmed by rumours of imminent invasion from Scandinavia.

For the English, the Norman Conquest was a disaster which brought in its train a social upheaval unparalleled in English history. The aristocracy was replaced by a baronage which was French, and largely Norman. The landowning classes were dispossessed, and those who survived the carnage of battle were socially and economically depressed, becoming in many cases the tenants of those Normans who had acquired their lands.

French became the language of the court, Latin the formal language of the church and of diplomacy, while English, which had been the vehicle of a flourishing vernacular culture, became merely the language of a conquered people, despised as they were despised, and forced into neglect.

How did the Norman Conquest of England affect Wales? Within five years of the battle of Hastings, the Normans were settled in strength along the frontier between England and Wales, and had begun to probe and to infiltrate Wales. For the next fifty years they would raid and settle over wide areas of Wales, now firmly ensconced, now driven back by Welsh resistance. In the end, they did not achieve a conquest of Wales comparable with their devastating success in England, but they created a complex of Anglo-Norman lordships which permanently changed the political and social character of Wales. This book is concerned with the impact of the Normans on Wales. How was it done? How did the whole process of Norman attack and settlement affect Wales in the Middle Ages? Above all, who were the Norman conquerors, and what brought them into Wales? These are the basic questions which I have tried to answer.

The beginnings of the story are easy to trace, but what of the end, if end there was? Two factors will help to determine a rough and ready means of limiting the story. The first is that between 1169 and 1171 a powerful group of marcher lords from south Wales found a new outlet for their energies. They became deeply involved in the conquest of Irish kingdoms and acquired other interests across St. George's Channel. This was, in fact, a move away from the interests in Wales which made the lords of the southern march restless and dangerous neighbours for the Welsh. The second is that as the twelfth century drew to a close, new and powerful Welsh rulers emerged, the Lord Rhys in south Wales and, in the next generation, Llywelyn ab Iorwerth in north Wales. This set the stage for a new phase of Welsh history. The central feature of the story would then be the attempts of Welsh princes in the thirteenth century to consolidate power and to build in the Principality of Wales a political structure capable of survival. With their splendid, though unsuccessful, effort, we shall not be concerned.

Within these limits of time we can watch the Welsh princes reel under the impact of Norman attack, but, unlike their English counterparts in the eleventh century, they did not go under. Despite heavy losses, Welsh power survived. The cost was great, for Wales became a patchwork of Welsh and Norman lordships. In the end, after two hundred years of survival, it would take the sustained attacks launched by Edward I to destroy Welsh political power and to complete the conquest of Wales.

Chapter One

Wales before the coming of the Normans

Medieval Wales was made up of a number of kingdoms or principalities which, from time to time, were drawn together under the control of a single powerful ruler. Hywel Dda (918-949/50) had brought about such a temporary cohesion in the tenth century. After long and bitter conflicts, another Welsh prince, Gruffydd ap Llywelyn, brought the whole of Wales under his sway in the eleventh century. From 1039, when he first appeared as ruler of Powys and Gwynedd, until his death in 1063, his principal ambition was to rule a united Wales. He fought for many years to overthrow two princes of Deheubarth, Hywel ab Edwin and Gruffydd ap Rhydderch. Very little is known about either of them, but they defended the independence of their kingdom with vigour and success. Only with the death of Gruffydd ap Rhydderch in 1055 did the northern prince realise his ambition and become effective ruler of the south (See figure 1). It had taken him sixteen years, and there were enemies in south Wales who resented his power. He experienced what was the common fate of many of the greatest princes of medieval Wales; he grasped the importance of a united Wales, but he could not persuade those who accepted his authority that unity and submission to one powerful king were desirable political aims. The fierce independence and proud spirit of the local princes were too strong. For the last eight years of his life, Guffydd ap Llywelyn dominated the whole of Wales. There is no evidence that he built up institutions of government, or that he was a statesmanlike ruler. His power was personal, and the traditions which survived in the Welsh Marches suggest that he was ruthless and unscrupulous in removing any who might challenge his authority.

How and why, then, was his power broken? The answer to that question lies in the complexity of Anglo-Welsh rivalries. Gruffydd ap Rhydderch, as ruler of Deheubarth, found ample opportunities for rich plunder along the frontier between England and south Wales. Gloucestershire and Herefordshire were border shires, and while Edward the Confessor ruled England the defence of these shires was weak and ineffective. Gruffydd and his brother Rhys raided these shires and carried off prisoners and booty. As soon as he had conquered Deheubarth, Gruffydd ap Llywelyn adopted the same policy towards England. He increased the pressure on Gloucestershire and Herefordshire, and the Welsh raids became more serious and their effects more devastating. The town of Hereford suffered severely. It was over-run in 1055, when the newly built cathedral was destroyed. But this was only one episode in a long succession of border incidents, each of which was costly. The English administration tried many expedients. They tried the hazardous experiment of adopting tactics which worked very well in France, building castles in Herefordshire and in the neighbouring county of Shropshire, and training men to fight on horseback like continental knights. When it was put to the test it failed, probably because the soldiers were not sufficiently well-trained in these new methods of fighting. Then a different approach was tried. A new bishop of Hereford was appointed, Leofgar, and although he was a cleric he lived and acted as if he were a secular magnate, and clearly he had some skill as a fighter. He gave great offence to churchmen by refusing to shave off his moustache, which was at once a symbol of his manhood and his military calling. When he was made bishop, Leofgar took the initiative and led an army into Wales in an attempt to surprise Gruffydd ap Llywelyn. It was a bold move, but it failed, for Gruffydd's men were ready, and the English force was cut to pieces. To repair the damage, the responsibility for defence was then entrusted to Aldred, bishop of Worcester, one of the ablest magnates at the English court.

These events demonstrated beyond all doubt the serious nature of the Welsh threat, and made it clear that a major effort would be necessary to contain, if not to destroy, the Welsh leader. At the time, the most powerful magnate in England was Harold, earl of Wessex. His sister, Edith, was the wife of Edward the Confessor, and he was the king's chief adviser. In the winter season of 1062-3, about Christmas time, Harold sent a raiding party from Gloucester on the long and difficult journey to Rhuddlan, where Gruffydd ap Llywelyn had a palace. They surprised and captured his hall, but Gruffydd escaped by sea. Then, in the summer of 1063, Harold and his brother, Tostig, set out on a campaign by sea and land to destroy Gruffydd. This time there was no chance of escape, and Gruffydd was driven into mid-Wales. Once he was beyond the borders of Gwynedd and Powys he was in danger; he was killed by Welsh enemies, and his head was carried in triumph to King Edward. It was a sad end for a very distinguished prince, and the *Brut y Tywysogyon* records a lament:

> [1063] was the year of Christ when Gruffudd ap Llywelyn was slain, after innumerable victories and taking of spoils and treasures of gold and silver and precious purple raiment, through the treachery of his own men, after his fame and glory had increased and after he had aforetimes been unconquered, but was now left in the waste valleys, and after he had been head and shield and defender to the Britons.

His aim had been to unite Wales, but he was deflected from the task of consolidating his control of Wales by the prospect of rich and easy plunder along the English border. The temptation cost him his life, and destroyed the brief unity which he had imposed on Wales.

The remarkable thing is that only three years before the Normans landed in England, Wales was still united, and there was every indication that the king of England would continue to face a strong and dangerous Wales for many years to come. The change brought about by the defeat and death of Gruffydd ap Llywelyn in 1063 was sharp and dramatic. Wales was once more broken up into its separate kingdoms, governed by different rulers. In north Wales two brothers emerged as the

15

leading figures, the sons of Cynfyn ap Gwerstan: Gwynedd was ruled by Bleddyn until his death in 1075, and Powys by Rhiwallon, who died five years earlier. They gave their allegiance to Edward the Confessor and ruled as client-kings, but this did not prevent them from pursuing forceful policies within Wales. After the Norman invasion of England, they formed an alliance with the men of the west midlands which might have proved dangerous to the Conqueror. Neither Bleddyn nor Rhiwallon was a negligible figure, but they were not men of the mould of Gruffydd ap Llywelyn. In south Wales, representatives of dynasties which had been overthrown by Gruffydd ap Llywelyn were restored to power, but, again, the men who came to the fore were lesser men. Maredudd ab Owain ab Edwin, of the house of Hywel ab Edwin, governed Deheubarth, while Caradog ap Gruffydd ap Rhydderch retained a minimal influence in the eastern territory of Gwynllŵg. For the next twenty years, they and their successors were challenged by rival claimants, and there was intermittent warfare and dynastic strife until, in 1081, the battle of Mynydd Carn produced a clearer and simpler arrangement of dynastic power in Wales.

In these circumstances, Wales was in no condition to meet the challenge of the Norman invasions. Perhaps men looked back with nostalgia to the great days of Gruffydd ap Llywelyn: who can say? Certainly, they faced aggression and greed from their new Norman neighbours while at a serious disadvantage, and the Normans, on their part, could exploit all the weaknesses and internal divisions of the Welsh. Wales needed leaders of outstanding ability, and eventually, in Rhys ap Tewdwr of Deheubarth and, a little later, Gruffydd ap Cynan of Gwynedd, they found princes capable of checking the Norman advance. Their hour of greatness lay in the future and, before they were firmly established in their territories, the Normans were to reap a rich harvest in their first spectacular advances into Wales.

When William of Normandy landed in England he was, as he asserted, claiming a kingdom which was his by right of inheritance. Edward the Confessor had named him as his heir, and the Norman duke was wresting from the hands of the usurper,

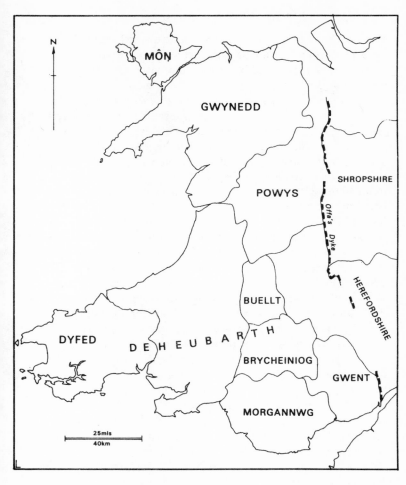

FIGURE 1
Wales in the time of Gruffydd ap Llywelyn

Harold, the crown which belonged rightfully to himself. That is an over-simplification of a sequence of events extending over fifteen years before the Norman Conquest, but, basically, it represents William's case. His primary concern was, therefore, to control the Confessor's kingdom as speedily as possible. From their base at Pevensey (Sussex), the Normans moved to Hastings, and then through Dover to Canterbury. They circled around London waiting for the submission of the English leaders. In the earliest years of their conquest they extended the range of their activities, from south-east England towards the outer limits of the kingdom. The full measure of their advance can only be seen on those occasions when they were challenged. In 1068, Exeter, in the extreme south-west, defied the Normans, and the Conqueror led an army to besiege and reduce the city. He established a castle there, and placed it in the hands of a trusted supporter. He also set up in the south-west his half-brother, Robert, count of Mortain, in order that the western-most part of his kingdom should be brought firmly under Norman control. The greatest point of danger lay in the north, and the Normans soon grasped, if they had not already known it in advance, the strategic importance of York. They made re-peated efforts to hold the city, but only after 1070 could they feel any real sense of security there. Gradually, a series of castles was established in the north, at such centres as Richmond and Pontefract, and the wild countryside of the Yorkshire wolds was slowly tamed. Further north still, the Normans found it exceedingly difficult to make their authority real, and Durham remained an outpost and a place of danger.

When it came to the Welsh frontier, however, the Normans had clear intentions and a precise policy. They were well informed about conditions in this border area, but their information was not up-to-date. They had obviously had reports of the succession of border raids and engagements which were characteristic of the 1050s and 1060s, but they do not seem to have realised the importance of Harold's victory in 1063, or of the death of Gruffydd ap Llywelyn. Perhaps con-temporaries could not be expected to see how sweeping and final those events were to be. Anticipating trouble, the

Normans established trusted magnates on the Welsh border. The necessity for a strong garrison was made clear in 1067 and 1069, when English patriots under their leader, Eadric the Wild, threatened the Norman hold over midland England and made common cause with Bleddyn of Gwynedd and Rhiwallon of Powys. The Conqueror crushed the English dissidents, and the Welsh were prevented from building up any long-term alliance by the frontier policy he now adopted.

Chapter Two

The first generation of settlers in Wales

The men appointed to control the Welsh frontier were carefully chosen. In the south, William fitz Osbern was established as earl of Hereford. Another magnate from one of the great families of Normandy, Roger of Montgomery, was given the central section of the border to guard as earl of Shrewsbury. In the north, Gherbod, one of William I's Flemish supporters, was made lord of Chester. Very soon he returned to Flanders, where he became involved in local family feuds, and he disappeared from the English scene. In his place, William appointed Hugh of Avranches as earl of Chester. William fitz Osbern, Roger of Montgomery, and Earl Hugh were all drawn from families with direct experience of the frontier between Normandy and the neighbouring French territories. Breteuil, the centre — or *caput* — of the fitz Osbern lordship, was strategically important. Bellême, held by Roger of Montgomery, who had inherited it from his mother, was pre-eminently a border lordship of Normandy. Hugh of Avranches was hereditary *vicomte* of the Avranchin, that part of Normandy which marched with Brittany. The *vicomte* resembled the English sheriff, and Hugh and his family were responsible for an area particularly sensitive to border rivalries. King William could scarcely have chosen better men, for they all knew at first hand what the defence of the frontier would involve.

William fitz Osbern was a Norman magnate of the first rank, for both his parents were descended from the Norman ducal house. His father, Osbern, was one of the guardians of the young Duke William during his turbulent minority, and he died by violence. As a young man, William fitz Osbern served the duke, and from about 1050 until 1066 was a leading figure at the ducal court. It is said that when some of the Norman barons argued against the proposal to invade England, William fitz Osbern won them over by his eloquence. In England he ranked as one of the half-a-dozen greatest secular magnates in the kingdom, and if there was serious trouble he could be relied upon to deal with it. He held the Isle of Wight and part of the coastal shire of Sussex, both danger-spots in the newly conquered country. He was to be found at York when the pressures there were at their worst. His skills were those of a fighting-man, not an administrator, and when he was left as joint-regent with Odo, bishop of Bayeux, in 1067, he earned an unenviable reputation for condoning brutality and harshness.

As early as 1067, William fitz Osbern was to be found at Hereford, organising the defences of the Welsh border. In Herefordshire itself he stood in the place of the king. His authority was less clearly defined but still very great in Gloucestershire, and he had considerable power in Worcestershire. He held many estates in Oxfordshire, and may have had some kind of official authority there too. The remarkable thing about him is that his career in England was very short, yet he managed to achieve a great deal. He went to Flanders early in 1071 to protect the interests of his ward, the young count of Flanders, and he was killed at Bavanchore, near Cassel, in February of that year. Fitz Osbern was described as 'the bravest of the Normans, renowned for his generosity, ready wit, and outstanding integrity'. In less than five years he had imprinted his mark on the Welsh border, and the effects of his activities were to be felt for many years to come. While his older son took the Norman possessions, his younger son, Roger, succeeded to his English estates; he seems to have been an unpleasant, truculent man. He was not allowed to exercise the wide powers entrusted to his father, and he resented the fact that the king's officials were at work in shires which he believed to be his own. In 1075 he was deeply implicated in rebellion against the Conqueror, and he spent the rest of his life as the king's prisoner.

Roger's sons lived in obscurity at the court of King Henry I, and only by marriage into the border family of Ballon did his successors retain some standing in the aristocratic society of England in the twelfth century. The great days of the family were over long before the death of William the Conqueror. The chronicler Orderic Vitalis was aware that William's grandsons, Reginald and Roger, had become 'some of the best soldiers in the service of King Henry; and are still awaiting his pardon which seems to them in their bitter conflicts too long delayed'. He viewed the fall of this dynasty with something approaching fatalism:

> Truly the glory of this world falls and withers like the flower of grass: even as smoke it fades and passes. Where is William fitz Osbern, earl of Hereford, regent of the king, steward of Normandy, and gallant leader in battle? He indeed was the first and greatest oppressor of the English, and harshly supported a huge following, which caused the ruin and wretched death of many thousands. Verily the judge sees things and rewards each one according to his deserts. For alas! see how the brave warrior William fell and received just retribution. He who slew many by the sword himself perished suddenly by the sword. And within five years of his death the spirit of discord moved his son and son-in-law to rebellion against their lord and kinsman . . . See now, I have truthfully related the crime for which the whole progeny of William was obliterated in England so thoroughly that, unless I am mistaken, they no longer possess a foot of English ground.

Roger of Montgomery was another great magnate, closely connected with the ducal house, who was one of Duke William's leading advisers. He married Mabel, of the family of Bellême, a name of notorious repute both before and after the Conquest. When Duke William set out for England in 1066 he left his wife in nominal control of the duchy of Normandy, and Roger of Montgomery stayed with her in Normandy as regent. Once he reached England, Roger was made responsible for a large part of Sussex, with its vulnerable coast-line, and by 1071 he had been made earl of Shrewsbury, with control over the middle section of the Welsh frontier. Earl Roger lived until 1094. He had a large family, and most of his sons became powerful and influential men.

Just what kind of men these Norman barons were is best exemplified in the accounts which the writer Orderic Vitalis has given us. Orderic was born near Shrewsbury in 1075, and when he was ten years old his father sent him to Normandy and dedicated him to the life of a monk in the monastery of St. Evroul. There he lived for more than fifty years, filling much of his time by writing. His most important book was his *Ecclesiastical History,* which occupied him at intervals for thirty years. Throughout his life he retained a strong affection for the Welsh border, but he was also a great admirer of the Normans, especially of those who were patrons of his own monastery.

Of Hugh of Avranches, earl of Chester, the third great lord of the border, Orderic says:

> Hugh was not merely generous but prodigal. He took with him as he travelled an army, not a household. He kept no account of what he gave or received. Each day, as he hunted, he laid waste his lands, for he valued fowlers and hunters more than those who tilled the soil or prayed.

Hugh was as undisciplined in his appetites as in his hunting, as his soubriquet, Hugh the Fat, implies. He was also 'always in the forefront of battle', and his other nick-name was Hugh the Wolf, a name with a deservedly ominous ring. Hugh lived until 1101, a terrible enemy, and a scourge of the Welsh for some thirty years.

In the early years of the Conqueror's reign, Norman forces were concentrated in strength on the Welsh border, and within a year or two of the Conquest the first Norman probes were being made in south Wales. William fitz Osbern set out to attract men to serve with him on the frontier and to settle in what was still a dangerous area. Anglo-Saxon towns had developed a body of custom by which the life and trade of the community were protected. These customs could be complex, and foreigners settling in a borough might justifiably feel confused both by the variety of the customs and by the penalties for their breach. To those who would settle in his frontier-town of Hereford, William fitz Osbern offered a simple and clear definition. The English burgesses of Hereford were to have all those customs which they had enjoyed before the Norman Conquest, but, as Domesday Book records, 'the French burgesses are quit for twelve pence from all their forfeitures'. Only three royal pleas were excluded from this concession, breach of the king's peace, housebreaking, and assault. In fact, Earl William gave to French settlers in Hereford the customs of his Norman borough of Breteuil, so that they could know in some detail how life in their new setting would be regulated. To those knights who were prepared to serve on the frontier, William offered similarly generous terms. There is a good deal of evidence that men of all classes of society were deliberately attracted to the frontier, and that they found social and economical advantages which were compensations for the greater dangers and hazards of frontier life.

Under the patronage of William fitz Osbern the first advances were being made into south Wales which were to lead to the founding of the first lordships of the March of Wales. He was responsible for establishing a ring of castles along the southern border: Chepstow, at the mouth of the Wye, still a gateway to Wales, Monmouth, Ewyas Harold, Clifford and Wigmore. They were at first simple motte-and-bailey structures, with earthwork defences surmounted no doubt by wooden palisades. The motte (o mound) was the main defensive point, while the bailey, wiu. its outer defences, provided a safe refuge and living quarters for the garrison. In most cases, the stone castles of which the ruins may still be seen, were built at a later date. Chepstow is exceptional, for there (as at Ludlow) stone defences were built in the eleventh century.

These earliest advances were made in the south. Two brothers, Maredudd and Rhys, the sons of Owain, successively kings of Deheubarth, and a third Welsh ruler, Cadwgan ap Meurig of Morgannwg, tried without success to stem the advance of William fitz Osbern's men. The Normans moved steadily into the coastal area of Gwent, into the cantref of Is Coed. Before his death, Maredudd had come to terms with Earl William and, through his influence, was holding estates in England. By 1086, when Domesday Book gives us a valuable glimpse of the southern march, the Normans were established as far west as Caerleon. There had also been some advance in another sector of the border, for the Lacy family had pushed their way into the territory long associated with their name, the lordship of Ewyas Lacy.

In point of fact, these advances from Herefordshire and Gloucestershire were less spectacular and less extensive than might have been expected. The explanation is clear enough. The death of William fitz Osbern in 1071 was a check to Norman initiative, and when his son was disgraced in 1075 the eclipse of this border family was complete. The king did not appoint another great magnate to replace the earl of Hereford. Instead, by a process which only slowly became apparent, prominent men who had served William fitz Osbern assumed a new status and new responsibilities. At the same time as the drive from the Norman side disappeared, the political situation in south Wales grew clearer. Maredudd ab Owain and his brother Rhys were much harassed by Caradog ap Gruffydd of Gwynllŵg, a vigorous and unpredictable leader. By 1078 a new name had come to the fore, Rhys ap Tewdwr, who strengthened his hold on Deheubarth, surviving a number of challenges and reverses. The disappearance of a strong Norman personality was matched by the emergence of a strong Welsh personality. King William found it useful to bind Rhys to himself as an ally, and his patronage was a further reason for south Wales's comparative immunity from attack until the 1090s. With the balance of power altered in this way, the Norman advance into the south-west was checked for some twenty-five years.

Roger of Montgomery was established on the border a few years later than William fitz Osbern, and here, in what would become the Middle March, the story was very different. Shrewsbury lay in the northern plain of Shropshire, facing the hills of the border, where English and Welsh had long struggled for dominance. One area had been under English control long enough to be an administrative unit, the hundred of Mersete, but its population was largely Welsh, and it had been captured and settled by the Welsh in comparatively recent times. The area around Chirbury had also passed under Welsh control. One of Earl Roger's first priorities was to regain these territories on the English side of the frontier. He gathered around himself an able group of lieutenants, and the task of consolidation was soon under way. The lordships of Caus, Oswestry and Chirbury were a new first-line of defence against the Welsh. The critical move, however, was the foundation of the new castle at Montgomery. Its earth-works may still be seen at Hen Domen (see plate 3, figure 5). To this outpost, thrust deep into the border zone, Earl Roger gave the name of his Norman castle, Montgomery, and from the castle a new shire would one day be named. Earl Roger has the distinction of being the only Norman magnate to give his name to a shire in England or Wales.

With Oswestry and Montgomery as key-points on the frontier, an aggressive strategy was inevitable. The process of reclamation and consolidation on the English side of the border gave way to a process of conquest and expansion in Wales. As Cynllaith, Edeirnion, Nanheudwy and Iâl were taken, the Normans pushed northwards and westwards from Oswestry. From Montgomery, Ceri, Cydewain and Arwystli were threatened and attacked. The advance into Arwystli drove deep into the mountain territory of mid-Wales, which spelled danger, not merely for Powys, the kingdom immediately affected, but also for Ceredigion on the west coast. It is worth emphasising that the interests of the earl of Shrewsbury extended far to the north. The commote of Iâl cut sharply into the territory where the earl of Chester was making his power effective, and as a practical solution to this problem the earl of Shrewsbury gave Iâl to the earl of Chester to be held under his own lordship. Such an arrangement was a rough and ready means of determining spheres of influence. There are signs that the Normans could be genuinely confused in Wales, as they were in England, as to the areas over which each might properly claim control. In Domesday Book, Robert of Rhuddlan was named as lord of north Wales, and one of the territories which he claimed in virtue of that grant was the cantref of Arwystli, captured and settled by men of the earl of Shrewsbury. It would need a bold historian to say accurately how much land the Normans actually held in these areas of advance. To indicate on a map the boundaries of

Arwystli or Rhufoniog should not be taken to imply that the Normans had advanced to the limits of these boundaries, nor that they controlled effectively the whole of the area.

The earldom of Chester survived long after Hereford and Shrewsbury had disappeared, and its history was closely linked with that of north Wales. Its name carries emotional overtones which have no place elsewhere in the Marches. When Hugh of Avranches became earl, he, too, established trusted supporters in key centres, like the lordship of Malpas. He was able to take full advantage of political rivalries in north Wales. The prince who would one day dominate the northern territories was Gruffydd ap Cynan, whose long struggle for mastery began as early as 1075. Nearly a quarter of a century passed before he achieved his ambitions. From 1075 until 1081 he had to fight a clever and resourceful opponent, Trahaearn ap Caradog, who was defeated and killed at Mynydd Carn in 1081. Then, just as he might have expected to reap the benefits of this victory, Gruffydd was trapped and captured by the Normans, and he spent many years—perhaps twelve, perhaps sixteen—as their prisoner. Only at the end of the eleventh century did he escape and re-establish his power in the north. He lived to be the most formidable of the Welsh rulers while Henry I was king of England.

Orderic Vitalis found it particularly difficult to be just to Robert of Rhuddlan. There was much in him which he admired, for Robert was a liberal benefactor to St. Evroul; he was a fine figure of a man, open-handed and generous. He was one of those Normans who were to be found in England during the reign of Edward the Confessor, and King Edward himself had made him a knight. But there was also much to condemn, for Robert could be ruthless and terrible, and nowhere was this more evident than in his dealings with the Welsh.

The warlike marcher lord (as Orderic reported) often fought against this unruly people and slew many in battle after battle. After driving back the native Britons in fierce combat he enlarged his territories and built a strongly fortified castle on the hill of Degannwy which is near to the sea. For fifteen years he harried the Welsh mercilessly, invaded the lands of men who

when they still enjoyed their original liberty had owed nothing
to the Normans, pursued them through woods and marshes and
over steep mountains and found different ways of securing their
submission. Some he slaughtered mercilessly on the spot like
cattle; others he kept for years in fetters, or forced into a harsh
and unlawful slavery.

Despite his admiration, Orderic could not but condemn all this
brutality. 'It is not right', he went on, 'that Christians should so
oppress their brothers, who have been reborn in the faith of
Christ by holy baptism.' He tried to find an explanation of
Robert's conduct. 'Pride and greed,' he decided, 'which have a
hold on the hearts of men everywhere, were the incentives that
drove the marcher lord, Robert, to unrestrained plunder and
slaughter.' But there was more to it than that. Robert was
following a policy of stern repression which, for many years,
maintained him and his men in command of his outpost. Cruel
and brutal it may have been, but it was neither aimless nor
entirely selfish.

In 1093, Robert of Rhuddlan was killed by Welsh insurgents
at the foot of the Great Orme. There was a heroic quality about
the manner of his death. As Orderic told the story,

> the Welsh king Gruffydd landed with three ships on the shore
> under the rocky height called the Great Orme, and the army of
> pirates scattered at once to prey on the coastal region like raven-
> ing wolves. Meanwhile the tide went out, leaving the pirates'
> boats high and dry on the shore. Gruffydd and his men swooped
> on the lands near the sea, carried off men and beasts, and
> hurried back to the boats lying on the beach.
>   Meanwhile the cries of the crowd roused Robert from a mid-
> day sleep, and made him aware of the hostile raid on his land. He
> leapt up boldly just as he was, and immediately ordered the
> trumpeters to summon his troops from the whole district. He
> himself, all unprepared, pursued the Welsh with a few men-at-
> arms, and from the summit of the Great Orme, a precipitous
> rock, saw the captives being bound by the raiders and bundled
> into the boats with the animals. The fury of the lord marcher, a
> man bold as a lion, knew no bounds, and he ordered the few men
> with him, all unprepared as they were, to fall on the Welsh while
> they were stranded on the beach before the tide came in. They
> protested that they were too few and the way down from the

summit of the rock too steep. Then Robert, seeing the enemy force waiting with the booty for the tide to carry them away, was sick at heart; unable to bear the delay, he flung himself down the difficult slope without his hauberk, accompanied by only one knight called Osbern of Orgères, and rushed on the enemy. When they saw him with only a shield for protection, accompanied by only a single knight, with one accord they flung their javelins at this valiant lord, bore down his shield with the weight of their missiles, and fatally wounded him. But as long as he remained standing and held his shield none dared come to close quarters or strike him with a sword. At last the noble warrior, riddled with darts, fell to his knees, let fall his shield as his strength gave way under the weight of weapons, and commended his soul to God and St. Mary the mother of God. Then all rushed upon him and, in full sight of his men, cut off his head and fixed it on the mast of a ship as a sign of victory. Many, weeping and lamenting bitterly, saw this from the summit of the hill, but they were powerless to help their lord. By the time their comrades from all over the province had assembled it was too late to give any help to the lord marcher, for he was already slain.

The most they could do was to give pursuit, and they were able to recover the head of their lord so that he could be given honourable burial. There can be no doubt that the Welsh knew full well the extent of the loss which they had inflicted on their Norman enemies. Robert was a scourge of whom they were well rid.

Earl Hugh of Chester acquired his cousin's possessions in north Wales. Under his leadership the Normans pressed hard along the coastal plain, building castles (of simple, basic construction) at Bangor and Caernarfon. They crossed the Menai Straits to Anglesey, and on the mainland they pushed down the Llŷn peninsula. At most, this can only have been a military occupation of the coastal strip. The Normans of Chester had neither the men nor the resources to attempt intensive conquest west of the Conway. Nevertheless, their presence was a real source of danger for the rulers and people of Gwynedd.

From the earldom of Shrewsbury, also, came a more adventurous move. Bold sweeps to the west coast had been made as early as 1073 and 1074. In 1093 the men of the earldom of

Shrewsbury travelled through Arwystli and struck westwards
to the coast. They gained a foothold in Ceredigion and established a stronghold at Aberteifi, which they came to know as
Cardigan. They did not attempt a full-scale conquest of Ceredigion, but continued their sweep south-westward into Dyfed.
There, with a new castle at Pembroke as their principal base,
they began to make themselves masters of the *cantrefi* of the
south-west, which became the lordship of Arnulf of Montgomery. As in the north, this bold sweep extended the resources
of the Normans beyond their capacity. Yet, in both instances,
they seem to have intended much more than a protracted raid.
Conquest was fragile, but the potential threat to the Welsh was
very great.

The scale of the danger provoked a reaction. It was certainly
no accident that the leadership of both Welsh and Normans in
north Wales passed into new hands. Gruffydd ap Cynan re-
appeared as a political figure in Gwynedd, while the death of
Roger of Montgomery, and the preoccupation elsewhere of
Hugh, earl of Chester, left the new earl of Shrewsbury, another
Hugh, as leader of the Norman forces. Driven back on the
mainland, and seeking to re-establish his hold on Anglesey,
Earl Hugh was killed in a skirmish with a Norwegian sea-borne
force. The result of these events was that in the north the
Conway was accepted as the limit of Norman expansion, and
Degannwy remained the outpost of Norman advance.
Gwynedd had won release from the fear of conquest, and
Powys enjoyed a respite. The time was not far distant when
Rhos and Rhufoniog would be regained by the ruling house of
Gwynedd.

The Norman hold in the south-west was equally tenuous, and
sustained assaults on Norman castles in Dyfed saw all but one
fall to the Welsh. The exception was Pembroke, a castle which
never fell to Welsh attack. Even so, the defence of Pembroke
during 1096 tested its castellan, Gerald of Windsor, to the limits
of his very considerable resourcefulness. What had been made
abundantly clear as the century drew to a close was that the capture and settlement of Norman lordships in the south-west

would be a matter for a later generation which would have little in the way of foundations on which to build.

The three marcher earls of the Conqueror's reign played an important rôle as patrons, for under their protection a number of prominent families were established in the Marches. In the south this process was interrupted by the eclipse of the earldom of Hereford, and it is not easy to penetrate through the period of obscurity which followed the events of 1071 and 1075. Along the southern March the Lacys were a major frontier family; so, too, were the Cliffords and the Mortimers. They were matched by the lords of Ewyas Harold, a family of English stock which survived the Norman Conquest. The Harold who gave his name to this lordship was the son of Ralph, nick-named 'the Timid', earl of Hereford. Ralph was a nephew of Edward the Confessor and a man of standing and influence. His son had to be content with much less in the way of landed wealth and social status, and it was as a border family that he and his successors made their name as lords of Ewyas. Such men emerged as the prominent figures along the southern March after the fall of the earl of Hereford in 1075, and some of them owed much to Earl William fitz Osbern. In the earldom of Chester the greater barons of the honour had their principal interests in England. They provided the earl with men and money for his campaigns, but only a small number had any direct interest in the March. In part, this was due to the dominant rôle played by Robert of Rhuddlan; in part, it was due to the fact that the advance from the north affected a comparatively short stretch of the frontier. It was an advance in depth along a narrow front. Apart from Robert of Rhuddlan, the lord of Malpas was the magnate most obviously involved in events on the border.

The earldom of Shrewsbury provides us with the best examples of frontier families established under the protection of the earl. For this, the simple fact that the earl of Shrewsbury was responsible for a long stretch of the frontier is explanation enough. When he wrote about the earl of Shrewsbury, Orderic could easily be led to digress, and to speak of his own family connections, but he drew a sharp picture of the earl surrounded by his leading supporters.

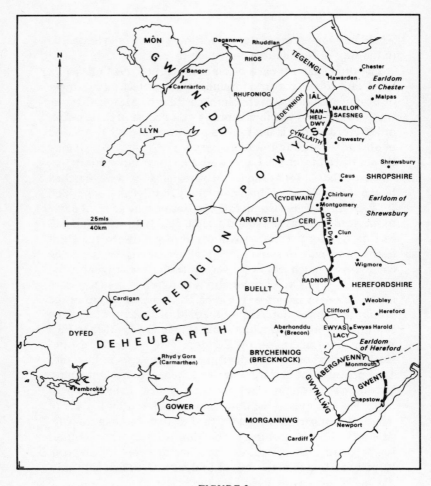

FIGURE 2
Wales in 1100

King William gave Roger of Montgomery first of all Arundel castle and the town of Chichester; and afterwards granted him the county of Shrewsbury, a town standing on a hill above the river Severn. He was a wise and prudent man, a lover of justice, who always enjoyed the company of learned and sober men. For many years he had in his household three learned clerks, Godebald, Odelerius, and Herbert, whose advice was very profitable to him. To Warin the Bald, a man small in body but great in spirit, he gave his niece Amieria and the sheriffdom of Shrewsbury, employing him to crush the Welsh and other opponents and pacify the whole province placed under his rule. He gave positions of authority in the county to William called Pantulf, Picot, Corbet and his sons Roger and Robert, and other brave and loyal men; and their judgement and courage helped to give him an assured place in the first rank of the nobility.

Odelerius was the father of Orderic, and was especially influential in securing the foundation of the abbey of St. Peter at Shrewsbury. Warin was particularly active in the advance across the frontier. When he died he was followed by Reinald de Bailleul, who was given both Warin's lands and his wife. From these estates the lordship of Oswestry grew into a recognisable unit. The Corbets, lords of Caus, were like the neighbouring lords of Clun and Oswestry; they were dynasties with a permanent interest in the March. Perhaps the most intriguing figure in this group of men was William Pantulf. He had been to southern Italy and had seen something of Norman expansion there, especially in the duchy of Calabria. Robert Guiscard, conqueror of that area, was anxious that William should remain in his service, and promised him rich rewards if he would throw in his lot with the Normans in the south. But William preferred the Welsh March. In fact, he ran grave risks by returning to northern Europe, for he was suspected of some share in a notorious crime, the murder of Mabel of Bellême, countess of Shrewsbury. The man who slew the countess was a close friend of William Pantulf, and he and his companions took refuge in southern Italy. So William was a compromised man. Happily, he managed to clear himself of suspicion and could continue to serve the earl of Shrewsbury.

Chapter Three

The Normans in South Wales

It is not easy to see why a second generation of Normans should have been attracted to Wales. Two new men in particular were to play an important part in the expansion of Norman power in south-east Wales. One was Bernard of Neufmarché (New-march), and the other, Robert fitz Hamo. Bernard was established in Herefordshire in the 1080s. He was from a distinguished Norman family which had fallen on evil days. His grandfather died by violence defending the interest of the young Duke William of Normandy. Then, in the next generation, Geoffrey of Neufmarché forfeited the duke's confidence and was disgraced. The family had custody of a frontier castle at Le Neuf-Marché-en-Lion, but the duke withdrew this charge from Geoffrey. Bernard seems to have set out to make his fortune in England, but it is only late in the Conqueror's reign, in the 1080s, that he can be traced holding land there. Marriage with an heiress brought him a modest estate, and by 1088 he had a number of manors in Herefordshire and had begun to advance into Wales itself. We must imagine him looking to the Welsh lands which lay beyond Hay and Glasbury, and then moving steadily into the heart of the Welsh kingdom of Brycheiniog. How deeply the Normans had penetrated into this kingdom, and how speedily they advanced we cannot know. What is certain is that their presence led to an appeal to the ruler of Deheubarth, Rhys ap Tewdwr, for help. He travelled east, and in 1093, he and 'the Normans who were living in Brycheiniog' met in a decisive encounter at Aberhonddu. There, at the confluence of the Usk and the Honddu, the Welsh king was killed. For Wales, his death had wide repercussions. The *Brut y Tywysogyon,* recording his death, lamented that 'with him fell the kingdom of the Britons'. South Wales was open to the attacks of Welsh and Norman enemies, but it was the Normans who made the greatest gains. They 'overran Dyfed and Ceredigion—what was not in their power before that—and made castles in them and fortified them'. The writer went on to say: 'then the French seized all the lands of the Britons'. For Brycheiniog, in particular, the Norman hold on the kingdom was strengthened, and their intention to secure this conquest was made clear beyond all doubt. Bernard of Neufmarché built his 'castle on the Honddu', as he called it, to be the centre of his lordship. There he was later to build his new borough of Brecon.

Bernard and his knights moved into Brycheiniog along the valley route from Hay towards Brecon itself, and they then turned towards the valley of the Usk to extend their conquests. To the north and south lay hills and mountains, heavily afforested land giving way to moorland. In the valleys, commanded and protected by castles like Aberyscir. Brecon itself, Bronllys, Tretower and Crickhowell, the new settlers could begin to build up a manorial organisation. In the upland areas the Welsh continued to maintain a pastoral economy. The Great Forest (of Brecknock) extended from the near neighbourhood of Brecon, south of Llanspyddid and Defynnog, across the mountain block of the Brecon Fannau towards the Carmarthen Fan. Here the lords of Brecknock could enjoy their hunting, while their Welsh tenants pastured cattle and sheep and took from the wild countryside the means of fertilising their lands, paying traditional renders in kind to their new lords. To indicate on a map which areas of the lordship were Normanised and secure, and which remained Welsh in loyalty would be no easy task. Talgarth, the ancient capital of Brycheiniog, Bernard retained in his own hands. Nearby, the Baskervilles held lands as leading tenants of the honour. At Bronllys the Clifford family (descendants of Richard fitz Pons) had a castle on an imposing site. Further away from the centre of the lordship, the castle of Hay defended one main route into Brecknock. It was held briefly by William Revel, but it escheated to Bernard as lord of the entire lordship. As the Normans advanced along the Usk, the Pichard family was established at Ystradyw, with their castle at Tretower. The gradual development of the castle on this site in the twelfth and thirteenth centuries, and the eventual replacement of the castle in the fourteenth century by a fortified manor house, presents one of the best architectural records of any fortified site in Wales (See plate 1). Beyond them, the Turbevilles had Crickhowell with its castle guarding the river-crossing. On the western boundaries of the lordship, the valley route through Llywel towards Llandovery opened the way for the Cliffords to advance from Cantref Selyf into Cantref Bychan, which lay beyond the boundaries of Brycheiniog itself.

Some of these dispositions were made soon after the conquest, while others were long-term developments. The castles were of critical importance, and before the end of the eleventh century their strength had been tested to the full. In 1096 Brecknock felt the impact of the Welsh reaction which had already affected many parts of the country. The Normans could not claim control over more than small areas defended by their castles. So much were they hemmed in that two attempts were made to send reinforcements and aid into Brecknock. The defeat of the second attempt at Aber Llech was certainly spectacular, for on their return towards safer territory the Normans were slain by the sons of Idnerth ap Cadwgan, Gruffydd and Ifor. But the Normans seem to have been able to strengthen castles, and perhaps to build new ones, as a result of this relief operation. With the castles securely in their hands, the Normans were capable of surviving the months of crisis. How quickly they began to restore order, how soon they could assert any control over the countryside beyond their castles, we cannot say. The early history of the conquest of Brycheiniog and of the creation of the lordship of Brecknock illustrates how fine was the balance between success and failure. In Wales, as in England, the crucial factor seems to have been the use of the castle as a refuge and as a base for aggressive action. The Normans might well be isolated in their new Welsh territories, but they did not lack in courage and resourcefulness, and the tactical advantage which the castle gave them remained a major asset throughout the eleventh and twelfth centuries.

South of Brycheiniog, the kingdom of Morgannwg was under attack during the last years of the eleventh century. The Norman lord who cast covetous eyes on Morgannwg was Robert fitz Hamo, a member of a distinguished Norman family. Like Bernard of Neufmarché, he came to prominence at a comparatively late date after the conquest of England, but in the reign of William Rufus (1087-1100) he was given a number of rich estates which had once belonged to a powerful Anglo-Saxon magnate, Brihctric son of Aelfgar. These estates passed, first, to the Conqueror's queen, and then to Robert fitz Hamo, and at a later date they were to form the basis of the great honour of Gloucester. There is no obvious reason why Robert should have become interested in conquests in Wales, but the port of Bristol, with its trade across the Bristol Channel, is the most probable link. The earliest stages of the conquest of Morgannwg are shrouded in mystery, and the obscurities were much increased by legendary accounts drawn up in the sixteenth century. The exploits of Robert fitz Hamo and his twelve knights are part of the mythology of south Wales!

The attacks on Morgannwg must belong to the same period as the early advance into Brycheiniog. We are presented with the fact of invasion, and to a large extent we must fill in the background with intelligent guesses. The attack seems to have been launched by sea. At least it is clear that the obvious land-route was not provided with adequate defence, which is a curious omission. The alternative explanations are that the Normans were extremely negligent, or that they did not rely upon this land-route. It is also increasingly clear that the earliest Norman occupation of Glamorgan, as they called their new lordship, was more in the nature of a foothold than an extensive conquest. They moved, perhaps somewhat hesitantly, from the coast in to the rich vale of Glamorgan, and the subjugation of this area was not speedily achieved (See figure 3). The hinterland and the upland area of the lordship were not touched, and only at a comparatively late stage were efforts

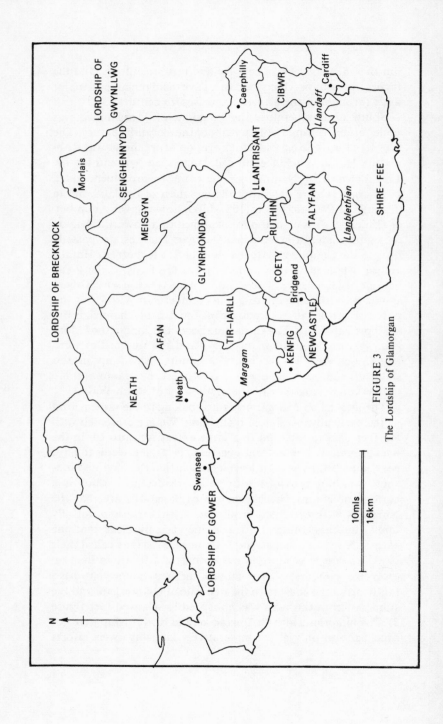

FIGURE 3

The Lordship of Glamorgan

10mls
16km

N

LORDSHIP OF GWYNLLŴG

Caerphilly

CIBWR

Cardiff

Llandaff

SENGHENNYDD

Morlais

LLANTRISANT

SHIRE-FEE

Llanblethian

MEISGYN

RUTHIN

TALYFAN

LORDSHIP OF BRECKNOCK

GLYNRHONDDA

COETY

Bridgend

TIR-IARLL

AFAN

NEWCASTLE

KENFIG

Margam

NEATH

Neath

Swansea

LORDSHIP OF GOWER

made to bring them under Anglo-Norman domination. The Welsh mountain lordship of Senghennydd produced stubborn and prolonged resistance to the advance of the alien settlers. The history of the lordship of Glamorgan reflects in miniature the history of Wales from the eleventh to the thirteenth centuries, a story of confused, turbulent, and changing relationships between Welsh and Normans, with some areas firmly controlled and settled, and with a comparatively late subjugation of the most stubborn outposts of Welshness. Morgannwg and Brycheiniog are reminders, if reminders are necessary, that the early conquests were areas of occupation, with a native Welsh population controlled to a greater or lesser degree by a small Norman minority. To speak of the lordship of Glamorgan is also to obscure the fact that two ancient Welsh kingships were involved, for the lords of Glamorgan also controlled Gwynllŵg, where their castle and borough of Newport became the main centre of Norman administration.

The focal point of the lordship of Glamorgan, however, was the castle of Cardiff, again with a newly-founded borough nestling under its walls. In 1107, the honour of Gloucester, with the lordship of Glamorgan, passed through marriage into the hands of Robert, an illegitimate son of King Henry I. Robert became earl of Gloucester about 1120, and the link between Bristol, the administrative centre of his English honour, and Cardiff, the principal castle and port of his Welsh lordship, was greatly strengthened. Much of Glamorgan remained under the direct control of the earl. Meisgyn and Glyn-rhondda were to become in the thirteenth century important demesne lordships of Glamorgan. Another large area in the western part of the lordship remained in the earl's possession, and came to be called the Earl's Land, Tir yr Iarll. All these areas came into the control of the lords of Glamorgan considerably later than the initial conquest in Morgannwg. Coety and Ogmore seem at one time to have been the western limits of Norman expansion, and the river Ogmore formed the boundary of Robert fitz Hamo's conquest. Grants which he made to St. Peter's abbey in Gloucester and to Tewkesbury abbey all lay to the east of the Ogmore. The three castles of Coety, Ogmore, and Newcastle

(Bridgend) have all the appearance of a defence for the border
of the lordship, while the primitive unity of this area of conquest is preserved in the area called the shire-fee, which remained as a permanent feature of the organisation of medieval
Glamorgan. At a later stage in the process of conquest, dependent lordships were established further west. A castle at Neath
commanded the western-most part of the lordship, and was for
a while in the control of the Granvilles. Afan (now dominated
by Port Talbot) was one of three lordships held by Welsh
tenants. When Caradog ab Iestyn received this lordship, he
seems to have grasped the value of the new-style organisation
which the Normans were introducing, and before his death in
1148 he had modelled his holding on the lordships held by his
Norman contemporaries. It was a rare example of a Welsh
leader adapting himself to the ways of the new men. It enabled
his dynasty to maintain Welsh control over a lowland lordship,
but there was a price to pay. Caradog's successors became
'Norman-Welsh', and adopted the curious hybrid 'de Avene' as
their family name. Their kinsmen, as lords of Ruthyn and Senghennydd, maintained a traditional way of life in their mountain lordships, where both the pressures and the temptations of
Norman influence were less serious and less persuasive.

Within thirty years of the conquest of Brycheiniog and
Morgannwg, south Wales had been overrun and settled. Some
areas, like Buellt and Radnor were occupied at an early date;
the Braiose family were already established there by 1095. They
held the English lordship of Bramber, in Sussex, and it may be
that their association there with William fitz Osbern, or more
probably with Roger of Montgomery, provided the impetus
which brought them to the Welsh Marches.

King Henry I, with his powerful deputy on the border,
Richard of Belmeis, bishop of London, was anxious to find for
Powys and Ceredigion Welsh princes who would maintain a
reasonable balance of power. Iorwerth and Cadwgan, sons of
Bleddyn, were each used as rulers not likely to disrupt the
Norman hold on Wales. Neither achieved great success, but at
least Powys was safe from large-scale attacks while the experi-
ment was being tried. They could not, however, hold in check

dangerous Welsh leaders, nor could they placate the Norman lords of the March. Cadwgan, especially, was much hampered by the recklessness of his son, Owain, who lived dangerously until he was finally trapped and slain by his mortal enemy, Gerald of Windsor, in 1116. The need for Welsh allies on whom the English king might rely was made the more urgent by the rebellion and overthrow of Robert of Bellême, earl of Shrewsbury. The rebellion, which threatened Henry I immediately after his accession in 1100, was put down, and two years later Henry was able to begin the process by which Robert of Bellême was rendered harmless. The earl was deprived of all his possessions and exiled from England, and the overpowering influence of his family in midland England and along the border was destroyed. So, too, was the power of his brother, Arnulf, lord of Pembroke. The *Brut* devotes one of its longest annals to these stirring events. (But the date given in this source is inaccurate, and needs to be adjusted.)

One thousand and one hundred (that is, correctly, 1102) was the year of Christ when there was treachery between Henry, king of England, and Robert, earl of Shrewsbury, who was called de Bellême, and Arnulf, his brother, who had come to Dyfed and had established the castle of Pembroke. And when the king heard that they were working treachery against him, he summoned them to find out the truth concerning that. But they sought pretexts to make an excuse, for they could not trust themselves to the king. And the king rejected their excuses after learning of their treachery. And when they knew that the king had learned of their treachery, and they dared not show themselves to him, they occupied their castles and fortified them, and summoned help to them from all sides and summoned to them the Britons who were under them, together with their leaders, namely, the sons of Bleddyn ap Cynfyn, Cadwgan, Iorwerth and Maredudd. And they received them with honour, and gave them gifts and promised them many things and gladdened the land with liberty. And a second time they fortified their castles and encompassed them with ditches and strong walls and prepared provision and gathered together knights and gave them gifts. Robert occupied four castles, namely, Arundel and Blyth and Bridgenorth—and it was against Bridgenorth that the whole treachery had been aimed, for he had built that without the king's permission—and Shrewsbury. Arnulf occupied Pembroke alone. And immediately after that they assembled hosts and summoned the Britons along with them and carried off spoils and returned home happy.

And while they were doing that, Arnulf thought to make peace with the Irish and seek aid from them. And he sent messengers, that is, Gerald his officer, and many others, to Ireland and he asked for the daughter of king Muircertach for his wife. And that he obtained easily. The messengers came back joyful. King Muircertach sent his daughter and many armed ships along with her to the aid of his son-in-law. And for that reason the earls waxed proud against the king, without wishing for peace or agreement from him.

And king Henry gradually gathered a host. And first he took the castle of Arundel. And thereupon through agreement and promises he gained possession of Blyth. And at last he came towards the castle of Bridgenorth, and with him a great host. And after surveying the castle from a distance he took counsel as to how he might capture the earl or subdue him or drive him out of the whole kingdom. And he resolved in council to send messengers to the Britons; and he summoned to him in particular Iorwerth ap Bleddyn, and he promised him more than he would obtain from the earl. And he gave to Iorwerth freely, without rent or payment, that portion of Wales which was in the hands of those earls, for his lifetime so long as the king lived; that was Powys and Ceredigion and half of Dyfed—the other portion was in the hands of fitz Baldwin — and Ystrad Tywi and Cydweli and Gower.

And when Iorwerth ap Bleddyn was going towards the king's castle, he sent his war-band to plunder the territory of earl Robert. And the war-band, cruelly and hostilely executing their lord's behest, gathered vast plunder and ravaged the land and pillaged it: for the earl had before that ordered his men to take their flocks and herds and all their chattels into the land of the Britons, for he placed trust in them, not supposing that he would meet with opposition from them, not remembering the wrongs that the Britons had formerly suffered at the hands of Roger, his father, and Hugh, his brother, and at the hands of their men, which was held in remembrance by the Britons.

Cadwgan, however, and Maredudd, sons of Bleddyn, were with the earl, knowing naught of that. And when the earl heard that, he despaired; and not trusting the help that was with him, because Iorwerth and his men had deserted him—for Iorwerth was foremost of the Britons and the most powerful—he sought a truce of the king to make peace with him or to leave the kingdom altogether.

42

Whilst they were about those things, Arnulf and his men had gone to meet his wedded wife and the fleet that had come to his aid. In the meantime, Magnus, king of Germany (correctly, of Norway), and with him a fleet, came a second time to Anglesey; and after felling for himself some trees for timber he returned to Man. And there he built three castles and a second time filled Man, which he had previously left desolate, with his men. And he asked for the daughter of Muircertach, king of Ireland, as wife for his son. And he obtained her easily and gladly. And he set him up as king over that island. And there he stayed that winter. And when earl Robert heard that, he sent messengers to him to beg help for himself; but he obtained none from him. And when the earl saw that he was besieged on all sides, he asked permission of the king to leave the kingdom; and the king granted it to him. And then he left all that was his and sailed to Normandy. And then the king sent to Arnulf and commanded him to go after his brother and to leave the kingdom or else to come at the king's will with his head in his lap. And when Arnulf heard that, he preferred to go after his brother than to submit to the king's will, and he surrendered his castle to the king; and the king sent a garrison to keep it.

And after that, Iorwerth ap Bleddyn made peace with his brothers and he shared the territory with them. And after a short while he seized Maredudd, his brother, and imprisoned him in the king's prison. And he made peace with Cadwgan, his brother, and gave him Ceredigion and a portion of Powys. And thereupon Iorwerth went to the king, thinking that he would have his promises from the king. But the king did not keep faith with him, but took from him Dyfed and the castle and gave them to a certain knight called Saer. And Ystrad Tywi and Cydweli and Gower he gave to Hywel ap Goronwy.

It was a tale of treachery and double-dealing, and the king, as well as the Norman lords of the March, was to suffer grave disturbance as a result of this settlement.

The departure of Arnulf of Montgomery left a vacuum in west Wales, but slowly lesser families began to reassert Norman power. Gerald of Windsor, who had served Arnulf as constable of Pembroke castle, emerged as a major figure in his own right, and the fitz Geralds were soon firmly established in the south-west. Another family which was to be prominent during the twelfth century, the family of de Barry, settled first at Barry in Glamorgan, and then at Manorbier in Pembrokeshire.

The river-crossing of the Tywi was a key-point; a castle had been established there at Rhyd-y-gors as early as 1095 by William fitz Baldwin, but it fell in the face of Welsh attacks in the following year. A decade later, in 1105, Rhyd-y-gors was rebuilt, this time by Richard fitz Baldwin. But this important strategic centre was not to be left in the hands of a marcher lord, nor did it long retain its original name. By 1109, the area was in the king's hands, and under the control of one of Henry I's experienced administrators, Walter of Gloucester. Henceforth, its principal stronghold would be known as Carmarthen, and it was to be the chief centre of royal influence in south Wales. Ystrad Tywi, Kidwelly and Gower had been entrusted to one of the lesser Welsh figures involved in the struggle for power, Hywel ap Goronwy, who was murdered in 1106. As the *Brut* tells it, the story was far from edifying.

> A year after that, Hywel ap Goronwy was slain through the treachery of the French who were keeping Rhyd-y-gors. And it was Gwgan ap Meurig, the man who had nurtured a son of Hywel's, and the man in whom Hywel placed greater trust than in anyone, who deceived him. For he invited him to his house and thereupon sent to the French in the castle and informed them of the night and what place. And they came by night about cock-crow and surrounded the hamlet and the house and raised a shout around the house. At that shout Hywel vigorously arose from his slumber and sought his arms and called upon his comrades and sought his sword, which he had placed above his head, and his spear, which he had placed below his feet. But Gwgan had removed them while he was asleep. And when Hywel sought his comrades and thought that they were ready to fight along with him, they had fled at the first shout. And then he too fled. And Gwgan pursued him and did not give him up until he caught him, as he had promised the French. And after Gwgan's comrades had come to him they strangled him. And after he had been strangled until he was well-nigh dead, they brought him to the French. And the French cut off his head and took it to the castle.

Another of the powerful administrators at Henry I's court, Roger, bishop of Salisbury, was soon established in Kidwelly.

only to be succeeded by the lord of Ogmore, Maurice of London (de Londres). Henry of Newburgh, earl of Warwick, acquired Gower. So the list might be continued, with well over a score of lordships established all along the south coast.

One family was certainly to rank among the greatest of the Norman lords of the March in the twelfth and thirteenth centuries, and that was the family of the Clares. Two branches of this family were involved in Wales. The senior branch appeared on the Welsh scene at an early date, was almost completely eclipsed, and then made a remarkable re-entry to secure a dominant place in marcher society in the thirteenth century. The cadet branch, meanwhile, built up a formidable nexus of power throughout the twelfth century. The history of the senior branch is closely linked with the early Norman infiltration into Ceredigion. At the beginning of the twelfth century Cadwgan ap Bleddyn and his son Owain held uneasy and broken sway over Ceredigion. Cadwgan was nominally *arglwydd* (or lord), while Owain was a wild, undisciplined fighter who, in political terms, was more of a nuisance than an asset to his family. The havoc which he caused in the west culminated in the abduction of Nest, the Welsh wife of Gerald of Windsor. It was an insult for which Gerald exacted full vengeance in due course. Within a short space of time, Owain was also responsible for the death of William of Brabant, a leading figure in the Flemish colony which Henry I had established in Pembrokeshire. In retribution, the king gave Ceredigion to Gilbert fitz Richard in 1110. Gilbert was already lord of Clare and Tonbridge, and his appointment brought a wealthy and powerful dynasty into prominence in Wales. Gilbert and his men had to win and hold Ceredigion, and he attracted settlers into the area. In the *Brut,* they are described as Flemings and Saxons. The Flemings are better known in south Pembrokeshire, where they were established by Henry I, and where they acquired the reputation of being hardy and determined men of the frontier. That English peasant settlers were attracted into the lands of conquest in the wake of Norman knights can scarcely cause surprise. To see how precarious was Gilbert of Clare's hold on Ceredigion, we cannot do better than turn again to the *Brut y Tywysogyon.*

And then (as the chronicler records for 1116), when Gruffudd ap Rhys came to Ceredigion, he came first to the place called Is-Coed and the spot which belonged to Gilbert fitz Richard, with Flemings dwelling in it, and which was called Blaen-porth. And that he attacked first. And on a certain day he besieged the tower throughout the day; and many from the tower were slain, and one of his men too was slain, and he burned the greater part of the town, without gaining anything but that. And then he turned back. Thereupon the men of the land as it were suddenly gathered to him, and they harried the Saxons whom Gilbert had brought in to fill the land, which was before that as it were empty because of a scarcity of people and well-nigh deserted; and they plundered and despoiled them and burned their houses, and directed their course to a place called Penweddig. And they surrounded the castle of Ralf, officer to Gilbert, which was at the place called Ystrad Peithyll. And they laid siege to it and overcame it; and they slew many within it and burned it by night, and they encamped at the place called Glasgrug, about a mile from Llanbadarn, and did wrong to the church: for they carried off cattle from the sanctuary for their dinner.

There followed an exciting sequence of skirmishes and sieges. Ralf, whose castle had been burned, went by night to his lord's castle at Ystrad Meurig to ask for help. The first Norman castle at Aberystwyth was under siege, and in the hand-to-hand fighting which followed, it looked as if the French might be worsted. In the general mêlée, Welsh pursued Normans, but, in the end, the men of Gruffydd ap Rhys were beaten off.

And when the French from the brow of the hill saw those fleeing, they swooped down upon them and slew them without mercy. And then all the inhabitants of the land were dispersed throughout the lands nearest them, some with their animals with them, others having left all their chattels without care for aught save they should find protection for their lives, so that the whole land was waste.

Gilbert's eldest son, Richard is said to have been more concerned with his Welsh lands than with his English possessions. He was ambushed and killed in 1136, not far from Crickhowell, and if Gerald of Wales is to be believed, he paid the price of quite unforgivable negligence.

It happened a short time after the death of king Henry I, that Richard de Clare, a nobleman of high birth, and lord of Ceredigion, passed this way on his journey from England to Wales, accompanied by Brian de Wallingford, lord of this province [i.e., Abergavenny], and many men-at-arms. At the passage of Coed Grono, and at the entrance into the wood, he dismissed him and his attendants, though much against their will, and proceeded on his journey unarmed; from too great a presumption of security, preceded only by a minstrel and a singer, one accompanying the other on the fiddle. The Welsh awaiting his arrival, with Iorwerth, brother of Morgan of Caerleon, at their head, and others of his family, rushed upon him unawares from the thickets, and killed him and many of his followers. Thus it appears how incautious and neglectful of itself is too great presumption; for fear teaches foresight and caution in prosperity, but audacity is precipitate, and inconsiderate rashness will not await the advice of the leader.

Elsewhere, Gerald defends the value of trusting the men of the frontier, and he may have been glad to hear and record this cautionary tale of what happened when an English nobleman intervened. Whether a commander with even a slight knowledge of the ways of the Welsh would have treated them with such contempt is open to question.

In the next generation, Richard's sons showed very different interests. The elder, Gilbert, was made earl of Hertford in 1138, and seems to have been chiefly concerned with his English estates. The younger son, Roger, who succeeded him as earl in 1152, had time for campaigning in Wales, and he either built or reconditioned a number of castles at strategic points, at Ystrad Meurig, Castell Hywel, Aberdyfi, Dineirth, and Llanrhystud. In 1158, as the *Brut* records,

Roger, earl of Clare, though he was in haste to come to Ceredigion, nevertheless did not dare to come until Rhys had made peace with the king. And on the second day from the Calends of June (31 May) he came to Ystrad Meurig. And on the following day he provisioned the castle and took Humfrey's Castle and the castle of the Dyfi and the castle of Dineirth and the castle of Llanrhystud.

Roger was pitted against the powerful prince of Deheubarth, Rhys ap Gruffydd, and by 1165 he had watched his Welsh lands overrun, and, accepting defeat, he had withdrawn from the Welsh scene.

When he died in 1173, he was succeeded by his son, Richard, who held the earldom of Hertford from 1173 until 1217, and who was fully occupied with dynastic interests and family estates in England and Normandy. The Welsh interests of this branch of the Clare family were pursued sporadically and when they were abandoned the family had ample resources elsewhere. Then, unexpectedly, a dynastic marriage radically altered the position. Earl Richard married Amicia, second daughter of William, earl of Gloucester. It was a good match, though at the time it could not be foreseen that the marriage would bring a great increase in wealth and power to the Clares. Earl William's only son died before his father, so that when William himself died in 1183 his estates passed to his three daughters. The division of this inheritance was a matter of high politics, for one daughter, Isabel, was married to John, youngest son of King Henry II. The Gloucester inheritance was designed to provide handsomely for Prince John, and he was lord of the honour of Glamorgan. In 1199, John divorced Isabel, but he did not loosen his hold on her estates. One of her sisters had married Amaury de Montfort, and their son was allowed to have the earldom of Gloucester until his death in 1213. Early in the next year, Isabel was married to Geoffrey de Mandeville, earl of Essex, and he, too, became earl of Gloucester. All this while, Richard of Clare and his wife were spectators, watching while King John dealt with the Gloucester inheritance. In the end, Amicia survived to be the sole heiress to her father's estates, and in 1217, only a few weeks before he died, her husband, Earl Richard, secured her inheritance. Thirty-four years had passed since William, earl of Gloucester, died, and during that time his lands and his title had fallen now to one, now to another claimant. In the event, they passed to the Clares, and as earls of Hertford and Gloucester they were magnates of the first consequence. They were also, once again, marcher lords in Wales, this time as lords of the rich and well-developed lordship of Glamorgan.

The junior branch of the family built up a considerable power on the Welsh March before the male line died out in 1185. Gilbert fitz Gilbert was the younger son of that Gilbert who had been given Ceredigion in 1110. When he was a young man, he had little in the way of lands or wealth himself, though his close relatives were powerful men. His elder brother held Ceredigion, while an uncle, Walter, held the eastern lordships of Nether Gwent and Gwynllŵg. He himself was to benefit from Henry I's bounty in England, and he was to become a leading baron of the March in Stephen's reign. He succeeded his uncle in Gwent and Gwynllŵg, and he received from King Stephen the lordship of Pembroke. About 1138 he was made an earl, with the formal title of Pembroke, though he often used Strigoil (or Chepstow), the centre of his eastern lordship, as a popular style. These acquisitions made Earl Gilbert himself, his son 'Strongbow', and his grandson, another Gilbert, powerful and wealthy men. Their estates in England did not compare in scale with their Welsh lordships. Gilbert fitz Gilbert was a younger son who was fortunate to acquire a large landed holding in his own right. For him, Wales was the land of opportunity. When the last of the male line died in 1185, his estates passed to an heiress, and it was fitting that her husband should be another man who had made his own way in the tough world of Angevin politics, William Marshal. His name, too, was a name to be feared in the Marches at the end of the twelfth century.

Chapter Four

Englishry and Welshry

1. *The Agrarian Pattern*

It requires a most difficult exercise of imagination to appreciate the confusion and bewilderment which ensued as the Normans and Welsh tried to understand the very different patterns of society which each race took for granted. If there were great contrasts, there were also similarities. It is becoming increasingly clear that there were large estates in pre-conquest Wales, marked by complex organisation and by a range of duties and renders from which the lord derived considerable profit. Both the form of organisation and the language by which it was described are unfamiliar now, as they were clearly unfamiliar to the Normans.

The characteristic great estate was described in north Wales as the *maenol,* and in south Wales as the *maenor.* It consisted of a number of settlements scattered over a large area, sometimes thirteen, sometimes less. The law-codes suggest that, in Gwynedd especially, each commote had twelve *maenolau* with two unattached townships. Such precision is not reflected in those agrarian arrangements which can be traced in practice. In the two commotes of Arfon, where the pattern of the law-codes would require twenty-four *maenolau,* there were apparently only nine. Whatever the overall pattern was supposed to be, a number of individual *maenolau* can be described in some detail over a period of time ranging from the eighth century to the fourteenth century. Maenor Meddyfynych, in Carmarthenshire, was a great estate covering the same area as the parish of Llandybïe. In the north, an estate known as Maenol Bangor could still be described in the fourteenth century in terms which clearly indicate that it was, as its name implies, an ancient *maenol,* for 'it contained, in an area of about ten square miles, no less than thirteen contiguous townships, some inhabited by freemen but most occupied by bondmen'. Part of the land of such a great estate was apportioned among the kinsfolk as share-land, *rhandir,* which might leave a mark on the local place-names. Rhandirgadog, in Anglesey, and Rhandirmwyn, in Carmarthenshire, are obvious examples. A striking feature of the *maenol* is the number of slaves and bondmen who were tied to the estate; it is a feature reflected in Welsh society in the eleventh and twelfth centuries. When the cantref of Tegeingl was described in Domesday Book in 1086-87, half the population were either slaves (17%) or men of inferior status who were probably servile in origin (34%). Perhaps such a feature explains why, in 1110, Owain ap Cadwgan could raid Dyfed and, without compunction, ship his captives to Ireland to be sold into slavery.

The people who lived on the great estate, the *maenol,* carried heavy burdens. Their principal obligation was the payment of a food-rent, the *gwestfa,* consisting of a variety of farm produce. Part of the land was under crops, and flour and oats were an important part of the *gwestfa.* But the Welsh economy was a mixed one, with cattle and pigs and sheep. One detailed statement of the food-rent due from an estate included a horse load of the best flour, the carcase of a cow or an ox, a full vat of mead, oats, a full-grown swine, a flitch of bacon, and a large block of butter. In addition, there were practical services to be rendered: the *arglwydd* (or lord) or his agent must be housed and fed when he visited the estate, recruits and provisions must be produced for his warband, and there was an obligation to do building work. Later there would be added cultivation of fields where services would have to be performed in keeping with the demands of the season of the year. It was a complex system.

The main feature of the Welsh rural economy, mixed though it might be, was that it was largely a pastoral economy, based on transhumance, that is to say, on the use of different pastures at different times of the year. Cattle were traditionally the chief form of wealth, and they were grazed on upland pastures in the summer (the *hafod*), and on the protected, lowland pasture in the winter. The moorland and forest areas were valuable for grazing sheep and swine. How to define precisely what the community, and what individual members of the community, might claim was no easy task.

The modern historian may sit in his study and wrestle at leisure with such problems, using all the resources of place-names, law-books, charters, rent-rolls, and field studies as a guide. What can it have been like for a Norman lord and his clerics, faced with a strange people, strange customs, and a strange language? They grappled with the problems in Wales, as they did in England in the eleventh and twelfth centuries. The remarkable thing is that, at quite an early date, the Norman invaders made the attempt to describe and to understand what they found in England, and for some small areas of the Welsh border they extended the attempt to cover Welsh society and Welsh customs. The account of Gloucestershire in Domesday Book has some interesting entries relating to Welsh lands. Wasuuic the reeve had under his control 13 vills or townships, Elmui had 14, Bleio had 13, and Ithel 14, for which they rendered payments in kind. Then there is what seems to be another unit of thirteen vills: one was waste, and Walter the Crossbowman rendered one measure of honey and one pig for it; Berddig, the king's jester, had 3 vills; Morin, Chenesis, an unnamed son of Wasuuic, and Sessibert each had 1 vill, and Abraham the priest had 2; one more was in the king's alms and paid to the church two pigs and 100 loaves, with a measure of beer. These eleven holdings were all described as vills, a word used as the equivalent of the Welsh *trefi*. Then there were two carrucates held by the churches of St. Michael and St. David, and half a carrucate held by Beluard de Caruen. So far, the Norman scribes could achieve precision, and what they describe appears to be a group of *maenorau,* one of them described in detail. (There are hints of the same type of estate in Ballingham in Herefordshire.) But there were three estates which defied such precision, and these were described as pastoral settlements *(harduices)* for which their Norman lord wished to have 100s. Both description and valuation were difficult!

There was, undoubtedly, the same kind of confusion as the Welsh tried to understand the manorial organisation which the Normans introduced into the lowland areas of their new lordships. In the lordship of Ogmore stereotyped tenancies of twelve acres of land and half-tenancies of six acres implied a clearly defined scheme of dividing land. The lord's mills were fully organised and in use by 1140, and the implication is that only these mills should be used in order that the profits should go to the lord of the fee. Men were described as *rustici,* and rustics, natives or serfs would be the terms used to describe them in English. Carrying duties were demanded. Both indicate that a servile or semi-servile population was burdened with labour services. The lord of Ogmore could farm his own estates by exacting labour from his tenants and serfs, and he was running a demesne farm, a home farm, with a grange at Colwinston for storing the crops reaped from his lands. There is even a clear indication that large, open fields were in use and, perhaps most significant of all, they could be described not in Welsh or French, but by the English name, *Langelande.* Such definitions must have sounded strange to Welsh ears, and such services may have been both bewildering and humiliating. These manorial conditions extended over a surprisingly large area in medieval Wales.

It is no accident that in Norman lordships in Wales a sharp distinction was drawn between Englishry and Welshry. In the one, a manorial-type of agrarian community was established, and profits and dues could be assessed in terms which would readily have been understood in many parts of England. In the other, Welsh custom prevailed, and a pattern of agrarian economy long characteristic of Wales was maintained. Here, payments in kind predominated. Perhaps the clearest way to describe the difference between Englishry and Welshry is to say that the Englishry was an area of direct exploitation of all the resources of the land, while the Welshry was an area of indirect exploitation.

There is a danger that in such a brief summary, definitions and contrasts may be made sharper than, in fact, they were. Some features of the Welsh economy underwent subtle changes under Norman influence, for the society of the Marches was in no sense a static society. Some features—notably, for example, the extended family, the *gwely*—are now being recognised more clearly as characteristic of many parts of Europe; they were not confined to Wales alone. We have always to remember that we are dealing with systems which were capable of wide variation and which were modified as a result of contact between Norman and Welsh. Bold, simple, and unqualified assertions will indicate the main lines of development, but they will not necessarily recreate in detail the reality which the men of the Marches knew in the twelfth century.

The Normans valued few things more highly than forest areas, for these provided them with the hunting which was a favourite pastime, and with welcome additions to their food supplies. The monk who wrote the Anglo-Saxon Chronicle at Peterborough abbey during the Conqueror's reign said of King William that

> He preserved the hart and boars
> And he loved the stags as much
> As if he were their father.

Few of his magnates lagged behind him in their zeal for the chase. Forests like Fforest Fawr in Brecknock, or Machen, or Chirk were well-stocked and often hunted. Many religious houses benefitted, as, for example, did Brecon priory, from the tithes of all the hunting of the local lord. But there were economic advantages of a different kind. Timber for building and repair was always available, and in many lordships could be claimed as of right. Brushwood was useful for kindling. Pannage for swine, that is, the acorns and beech-mast of the forest, was a normal means of keeping herds of pigs, and the lord of the fee could exact his dues, usually one pig from a fixed number as part of the profits of the forest. Wild bees produced honey which was much prized, and renders of honey were a constant feature of Welsh communities. In the upland areas, where forest gave way to moorland, the right of turbary, that is, the right of cutting turves and peat, was much valued.

Again, it is no accident that, in the Marches, areas of Welsh settlement as opposed to Norman infiltration tended to be in the upland territories. Here animals could be grazed; here the scattered communities of Welsh families could live and find some scope for arable farming. In the lordship of Radnor, the Welshry occupied the high land in a broad sweep around the area of Norman settlement. In Brecknock the river valleys were marked by manorialised settlements, while the Welshry, again, contained them almost in a framework of upland settlement. The degree of submission which the Normans could exact from the Welsh might vary from one lordship to another, and from one period of time to another. The acknowledgement of lordship was marked by customary payments. *Cymorth* was originally an ancient render of cattle, and it was long continued as a feature of Welsh agrarian society. In some lordships it retained much of its old character. In others it underwent a subtle change and became a money payment in lieu of a variety of services and renders in kind. Another payment was *ebediw,* a heriot; at a man's death his lord could claim his best beast, or sometimes the second-best animal. *Amobr* was the equivalent of a fine for permission to marry. Perhaps the render which stands out most clearly as a symbol of the whole system was the development of an advowry rent by which a man acknowledged the authority of his lord in general terms. These payments are not importations. They are, rather, adaptations of customary Welsh renders which any *arglwydd* might claim. It would be wise to add that much of the evidence for the structure of Norman and Welsh society is drawn from later centuries, though the normal assumption is that this late evidence embodies long-standing features of Welsh society.

2. *The Castle in Conquest and Settlement*

The division between Englishry and Welshry was not easily

or willingly accepted. It was a mark of conquest, and it depended upon a system of defence which was continually in use. The *Brut y Tywysogyon,* that bloodthirsty record of a dangerous age, records some thirty-six occasions between 1070 and 1200 on which attacks were made on major Norman strongholds. Some were local in their repercussions, others national. A list drawn up from all the available sources would certainly record many more attacks. The Marches were an area in which war could flare up at any moment. Insecurity was the basic condition of life, and the Anglo-Norman settlers and the native Welsh population lived in a state of constant readiness.

The castle was the key to Norman success. Earthworks could easily be thrown up, and within a matter of hours a rudimentary 'castle' could be established. The Bayeux Tapestry shows English rustics building a castle-mound for their new Norman masters at Hastings (See plate 2). A few days could see an effective castle in being; a few weeks could see a formidable stronghold established. The earthworks might be very simple. There were many mottes (artificial mounds) set up as vantage points from which a small group of Normans could defend themselves. The normal plan for an early Norman castle, once the need for immediate defence had passed, was that of the motte-and-bailey castle. The motte, reinforced with wooden defences, was the real strong-point of the castle. The bailey (or courtyard) was at once a first line of defence and a protected area within which the garrison could live (See plate 3 figure 5). In the reign of Henry I, as Gerald of Wales reported, Arnulf of Montgomery built at Pembroke 'a slender fortress with stakes and turf'.

Wooden defences could be built upon the earthworks and the castle would be strengthened, though it became much more vulnerable to destruction by fire. If the soil was loose and shaly, and unlikely to bind well to make a firm foundation, the motte could be reinforced by encasing the lower part of the mound, that is, by revêtement. Where stone was easily available it might be used for this purpose, or as a hard core for the motte itself. The basic pattern was simple, and Norman troops could be in-

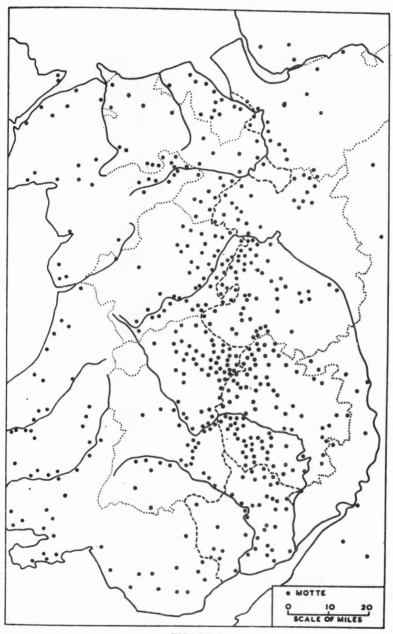

FIGURE 4
The distribution of mottes in Wales and
the Marches

genious in their use of local resources. Gerald of Wales told the story of two Norman soldiers caught up in a clash near a motte-and-bailey castle in Gwent. Pursued by the Welsh, they crossed a bridge to take refuge in a tower built on a mound of earth. Welsh archers used such force that their arrows penetrated the gate, made of oak beams four inches thick. The same kind of solid defences must have been built at Llys Edwin, in north Wales, where excavation has shown that the earthworks were strengthened by a palisade of heavy wooden logs, between seven and nine inches in diameter. Mottes and motte-and-bailey castles were built along the Marches throughout the late eleventh and twelfth centuries. Few can be dated accurately and in a number of cases excavation has failed to produce a range of artefacts to enable archaeologists to contribute greatly to our knowledge of these early castles.

Hen Domen, the old castle of Montgomery, has recently been excavated, and it is now possible to say something about its construction and about its relationship with the surrounding area. Over a period of about 130 years, from its foundation by Roger of Montgomery to the abandonment of the site as the primary defence of the whole area in the first years of Henry III's reign (1216-72), Hen Domen remained a castle dependent upon earthworks and wooden fortifications. It was constantly under repair. The ditch around the bailey was cleared and re-dug five times, so that the dangers which might come from allowing the ditch to silt up were avoided. The timber defences were altered in detail, and the buildings in use on the site were adapted from time to time and new ones added. There was a wooden hall, and in the latest phase of building at least, there was a wooden chapel, with the east end built in a half-circular apse, typical of many stone churches of the twelfth century. Perhaps the most interesting feature of this long process of repair and renewal is that no fewer than five successive bridges were built to join the bailey with the motte. The earliest rested on a massive sleeper-beam, 14 feet long and 10 inches square. As the years passed the defenders made sure of access to the top of the motte; time brought no respite. They rebuilt it on at least four occasions, sometimes even changing the angle of ap-

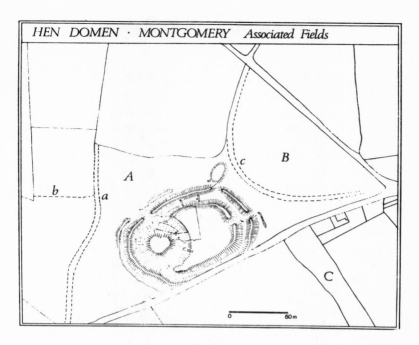

FIGURE 5
Hen Domen, Montgomery

proach from the bailey. The castle was kept in constant readiness, and to the end the motte remained as a last refuge easily and safely accessible. This old castle of Montgomery was not set up in a wilderness. It guarded a ford which was itself a critical point in the line of communication across the Severn, and it was established in an area where a pattern of pre-Norman fields has been traced. At the beginning of Henry III's reign, Hubert de Burgh began to build a new castle for the young king, on a bluff overlooking the approaches to Powys. The old castle became redundant, and Montgomery as a name was associated with the new castle, and with the borough which grew up below it. It is not clear whether the old castle was then used as an outpost, still depending on earthworks and wooden defences, or whether it was allowed to fall into disrepair, to be used for domestic purposes, perhaps with squatters living on the site.

The excavation of a castle at Penmaen, in Gower, also produced exceptional results, for here the type of timber structure which was in use has been identified. A large tower gate-house set in earthwork defences was the main feature of this stronghold. Hen Domen and Penmaen are valuable indications of what the archaeologists can teach us about early Norman castles.

A motte was easy to build. It might be used as a temporary defence, or as a base from which to attack an enemy stronghold. Such sites must have been abandoned as soon as their usefulness was over and may be regarded as campaign castles. Some mottes were thrown up in a hurry, only for their occupants to discover disadvantages which made the site unsuitable for permanent occupation. Lack of drinking water, or ground which rapidly became water-logged when rain swept over the Welsh hills—such reasons as these could well have persuaded Normans to leave an early fortification, and to move to a better site nearby. There is something of the order of 450 mottes or motte-and-bailey castles still to be traced in Wales and the Marches (See figure 4). The majority of them represent a first line of defence of Norman conquests in Wales, and an immediate place of refuge in time of trouble.

Within this network of defensive posts there was a number of key-positions where major castles were gradually built on a grander scale. In time, these key points would be defended by stone castles. The process of rebuilding in stone was well advanced in England. Stone defences were built in the twelfth century at many castles, like the royal stronghold at Dover, or the private baronial castle at Framlingham. There was also a number of the great stone dongeons which had been built in England since the time of the Conqueror. The Tower of London and Colchester are early examples; Bristol castle had a great stone keep early in the twelfth century. Henry II continued the tradition with such castles as that at Orford (Suffolk). Wooden fortifications were still to be seen at the beginning of the thirteenth century, and many of the surviving ruins of English castles indicate extensive rebuilding and extension in the thirteenth century. King John was replacing wooden defences at the city of Worcester with stone-built fortifications early in the thirteenth century, while at Shrewsbury, to cite another example, a great wooden tower was still part of the defences until the third quarter of the century, for it collapsed some time between 1269 and 1271.

The position in Wales is not so clear. There is not the same wealth of written sources to supplement the architectural record. In England the king's building activities left their mark on the records of the royal administration, but in Wales castle-building was the task of the local magnate. Stone defences dating from the eleventh century have been identified at Ludlow, in part of the curtain wall and its square towers, and at Chepstow. where a tower keep was the main feature of the early castle. There was a considerable amount of building in stone in the twelfth century. Some, like that at Ogmore, is believed to be quite early, and there are many castles where a date later in the twelfth century seems likely. At Kidwelly, apart from the mound, all traces of the early Norman castle have been obliterated by later building programmes. At Skenfrith, where there was certainly a stone-built castle in the twelfth century, by far the greater part of the castle which now survives in ruins dates from a period after 1216. At Brecon the impressive motte of Bernard of Neufmarché's castle survives, but all the surviving stone-work belongs to the castle which was such an important administrative centre in the later middle ages, and dates from a period well after the twelfth century. At Caus, the earthworks are much more valuable as an indication of what the early fortifications were like than the fragments of stonework which have survived. A contrast in building styles helps to distinguish the surviving twelfth-century work at Manorbier. There, by the middle of the twelfth century, a fine stone castle had been built, and there Gerald of Wales spent a happy boyhood. Manorbier, as he wrote in later life, was

> excellently well defended by turrets and bulwarks, and is situated on the summit of a hill extending on the western side towards the sea-port, having on the northern and north-western sides a fine fish-pond under its walls, as conspicuous for its grand appearance, as for the depth of its waters, and a beautiful orchard on the same side, inclosed on one part by a vineyard, and on the other by a wood, remarkable for the projection of its rocks, and the height of its hazel trees.

It was an idyllic scene, for the castle, though strongly defended, had become a pleasant place in which to live. As at Manorbier, so at White Castle; in this castle in Gwent there were certainly stone defences in the twelfth century. The castle of Bronllys, in Breconshire, is a round tower built in stone in the middle years of the twelfth century. In 1165, the lord of Brecknock was inspecting the site when he was killed by a fall of masonry from the tower. Cardigan, too, was being rebuilt in stone a few years later. The Lord Rhys captured the stronghold, and in 1171 he began to build a stone fortress there. Pembroke was the most formidable of these early castles, and from the beginning it owed much to the natural advantages of the site. With strong defences, culminating in the early thirteenth century in the finest round keep in Britain, it was a splendid piece of military architecture, and a symbol of Norman strength in the south-west.

Many castles fell to a determined assault. In the most celebrated incident of early border conflict, Owain ap Cadwgan captured the castle which Gerald of Windsor had at Cenarth Bychan and carried off his Welsh-born wife, Nest, and three of his children. When the outer defences had already fallen to the Welsh, the defenders could still hold out in the keep. Nest persuaded her husband to escape through a garderobe (or latrine-chute) built into the wall of the keep. Once he was clear, the doors were opened and Owain gained admittance to the innermost part of the stronghold. On another occasion, later in the century, Ifor Bach, lord of Senghennydd, raided Cardiff, scaled the castle walls, and carried off William, earl of Gloucester, with his wife and son. William was no soldier and contemporaries mocked him for his lack of manly qualities, but it must have been a humiliating experience, not only for him, but for the whole garrison of Cardiff.

In this sphere of fortification, the Welsh were able to do what the English never achieved, for they took over the Norman-style castles, and reaped for themselves some of the strategic and tactical advantages which these castles provided. There was a long-standing tradition of the use of hill forts, and the Welsh princes were ever on guard against surprise attacks from their neighbours. Because the process of conquest and settlement was so long drawn out the Welsh had ample time to adapt to new ideas. The leading princes of the twelfth century grasped the value of the new-style fortifications. The *Brut* records that in 1116 Einion ap Cadwgan and Gruffydd ap Maredudd ap Bleddyn came to terms with Henry I, and the upshot was an attack on Uchdryd ab Edwin. A significant detail was added, for they attacked the castle which Uchdryd had built at Cymer in Meirionnydd. In the 1140s Cadwaladr ap Gruffydd ap Cynan had castles at Aberystwyth and Cynfael, and in 1149 he built another castle at Llanrhystud. The same year saw his brother, Owain, building a castle in Iâl, and Madog ap Maredudd the castle at Oswestry, a centre which he held very briefly. So the story would continue for the rest of the century, with Welsh leaders repairing castles at Carmarthen and Ystrad Meurig, and building strongholds at Dinefwr, Humphrey's Castle, in the valley of the Cletwr, Caereinion, and Cyfeiliog. When Rhys ap Gruffydd emerged as the leading Welsh prince in the south, he, too, was responsible for a number of castles, at Aberdyfi and Rhaeadr and, where the Normans had once held sway, at Cardigan and Kidwelly. Some of these may have been temporary strongholds. In 1156, knowing that an attack upon him was imminent, Rhys 'raised a ditch'—clearly a ditch and bank defence—at Aberdyfi, and then built a castle there. Rhaeadr was built in 1177, and seventeen years later, in 1194, Rhys 'built it for a second time'. It was stormed and burned before the end of the year. By 1200 the value of fortifications was appreciated to the full, for in that year Maelgwyn ap Rhys earned general condemnation because, through fear and hatred of his brother, he 'sold to the Saxons the lock and stay of all Wales, the castle of Cardigan.' He compounded the felony by selling it 'for a small worthless price'!

Very few castles were impregnable. Pembroke was a rare exception, and Carmarthen could normally be relied upon to hold fast. Yet even Carmarthen, important royal centre though it was, fell to the Welsh in 1137 and was not recaptured until 1145. Shortage of supplies and reinforcements was a constant weakness for the Normans, who trusted that, in time of crisis, they could hold their castles until the troubles were over. Lack of experience in the proper performance of castle-guard made it less easy for the Welsh to hold a castle once it had been captured. A Welsh leader might deal effectively with one castle, or even with three or four main centres. But the large network of castles scattered throughout the Marches meant that no leader could penetrate the defence in depth and maintain heavy pressure on the Normans over a wide front. When that danger occurred, as it did, for example, under the Lord Rhys, royal influence and massive resources might be thrown into the conflict to the ultimate advantage of the marcher lords. In the long run the castle was an asset which served the Normans well. The Marches became pre-eminently 'the land of castles', and the Norman hold could not be dislodged.

3. The early boroughs

Another feature of Norman settlement which was to have profound repercussions for medieval Wales was the establishment of boroughs. Where a major castle was built, a small com-

PLATE 1

English peasants building a motte for Hastings Castle
under the supervision of a Norman (Bayeux Tapestry)

PLATE 2   Tretower Castle and Court

PLATE 3   Hen Domen, Montgomery

munity might easily grow. A garrison needs provisions, and a small trading community is, almost inevitably, the immediate consequence of military settlement. That could be demonstrated in this country from the relationship between a Roman camp and the civilian settlement which grew up outside its walls. Caerleon is a splendid example. It could be demonstrated equally well from India under British rule, for there the establishment of a military post was followed by the growth of a small and often vigorous Indian trading community just outside the army lines. This undoubtedly happened in Norman Wales. Towns were not characteristic of Welsh life, but it is no cause for surprise that a borough should grow under the shadow of a Norman castle. The advantages of trade, and the necessity of keeping open vital lines of communication with English ports like Bristol were an added incentive for the growth of the borough. That certainly is true of Newport and Cardiff, and to a lesser extent of Swansea. Bristol was the administrative centre of the great honour of Gloucester, and since the earls of Gloucester were also lords of Glamorgan, the links between Bristol and their Welsh strongholds at Newport and Cardiff were particularly important.

Similar factors affected the growth of Rhuddlan, where a small borough existed as early as 1086. To provide for the garrison of that key outpost, to encourage trade, and to keep open the sea-links with Chester, on the one hand, and a little later with Degannwy, on the other, these account for the early development of this borough. Since Rhuddlan was on the site of a princely residence of Gruffydd ap Llywelyn (1039-63), there may perhaps have been a small settlement at this strategic site before the coming of the Normans. Elsewhere along the frontier, that was certainly true. At Clun, for example, the Norman castle became the focal point of a small borough, but the church, which is some distance away from the castle, was the centre of a small, earlier settlement still clearly to be seen in aerial photographs. Swansea is the modern form of a Scandinavian place-name, Sweynseye, made up of the personal name *Sweyn,* and the topographical feature, *ey,* an island. That implies a recognisable place, though there is nothing to suggest that a settlement existed there before the Normans arrived. The motte-and-bailey castle, which has completely disappeared, was Norman; the earliest church on the site was Norman; and these seem to be the origin of the borough which developed in the twelfth century. Like Carmarthen, Cardiff was a Roman settlement, and there the remains of the Roman defences were used to good advantage by the Normans when they built their castle.

A Norman lord could encourage settlers in such a borough in two ways. He could offer them advantageous treatment in other parts of his possessions, so that their trading ventures were not hampered by tolls and charges. The earls of Gloucester gave such privileges and exemptions to their burgesses at Newport and Cardiff. More important were the conditions which a lord might offer in order to make a settlement attractive. By 1086 the burgesses of Rhuddlan had already been granted special favours. As Domesday Book tells us, they had been given the customs of Breteuil as they were in use at Hereford (See p. 24). There, at Rhuddlan, the citizens had a body of custom, easily identifiable and especially favourable, by which to trade, hold lands and tenements, and organise social relationships. At Cardiff, Robert, earl of Gloucester, had granted his burgesses a series of rights and privileges before his death in 1147. He embodied these grants in a charter which has not survived, but the terms of his concessions are known from a confirmation issued by his son, Earl William (1147-83). Every burgess owed an annual rent of twelve pence which covered all his services. He could dispose of his burgage, that is, his town property, as he chose. No lord could intervene and claim it, or direct how and where it should be sold. He could leave his burgage to his heir without hindrance. In feudal society, a lord might claim heriot, a payment due on the death of a tenant, or relief, a sum of money to be paid before an heir could enter into his inheritance. In Cardiff (as in most boroughs), neither of these payments could be demanded. In feudal society, too, when a man died and left a young son, a minor, as his heir, his lord could claim custody of the heir and of his estates, and could enjoy the income from those estates while the child was under age. In

Cardiff, the normal custom of a borough prevailed, and an heir and his estates were left in the care of his family, and not of his lord. In all, the burgesses were granted eighteen clearly defined rights and privileges. The men of Cardiff organised their lives on the basis of these customs throughout the twelfth and thirteenth centuries until, in 1284, they obtained permission to adopt the customs of Hereford.

The boroughs were always small. Sometimes, as at Tenby, the line of defence is clear, and the limits of the medieval borough may still be seen. For other towns we have to rely upon early pictures in order to see the extent of the medieval walls. The seventeenth-century cartographer, John Speed, added to his county maps plans of the principal towns. His plan of Cardiff, dating from 1610, shows the fully developed defences of the medieval town. A plan of Brecon, drawn up in 1744, shows plainly the line of the medieval town wall, a line still clearly marked in the street plan of the modern town.

The Norman boroughs of Wales lack the precise and planned layout of the Edwardian boroughs of a later age, nor were they ever part of an integrated defence system. They introduced into an agrarian economy a new element, and they contributed largely to the flow of trade, language and ideas in Wales and the Marches.

Chapter Five

Integration or Co-existence?

From the time of William the Conqueror to that of Rhys ap Gruffydd the fortunes of war changed markedly. If the Norman invaders could generally claim the advantage, there were periods when the Welsh achieved an unwonted degree of unity, and then the tide of success ran the other way. Rhys ap Tewdwr at the end of the eleventh century, and Gruffydd ap Cynan at the beginning of the twelfth century, or, in later years, Owain Gwynedd and the Lord Rhys, could make Welsh princely power effective over a wide area. Then, Dinefwr or Aberffraw might be names with which to conjure. Checked in 1098, the Normans never again extended their range of conquest in north Wales beyond the Conway. A century later, Rhys ap Gruffydd captured castle after castle in the south, and for a while it seemed that he might wrest from Anglo-Norman control a number of the principal lordships of south Wales.

At other times, when disunity and rivalry were the chief characteristics of Welsh society, the invaders could hope for success and expansion. It might be said that the conditions of peace, in which integration between Normans and Welsh might have occurred, did not exist. When war was endemic, racial conflict was unavoidable. Yet there were signs that the two races might grow together, and something recognisable as marcher society might emerge. Intermarriage offered some hope that this might be possible. From the beginning of Norman expansion into Wales, marriages between Norman and Welsh families were arranged. From the Norman side, such marriages seemed to offer a secure title to Welsh lands, though there was serious risk of misunderstanding the position in Wales. The Normans were developing into a firm legal principle the view that estates should pass from father to eldest son, and this concept of primogeniture as the key to inheritance made for permanence and stability in Anglo-Norman society. They did not grasp the fact that this concept was totally alien to Welsh traditions. From the Welsh side, such alliances may have offered the promise of immediate help in the conflicts between one *arglwydd* and another. Osbern fitz Richard married Nest, the daughter of Llywelyn ap Gruffydd, and their daughter was called Agnes. She also used the name of Nest, and presumably her mother maintained Welsh habits in her new home. Agnes, in her turn, was married to Bernard of Neufmarché, so that from the outset Norman and Welsh blood flowed in the veins of the lords of Brecknock. The most famous of these early mixed marriages was the alliance between Gerald of Windsor, castellan of Pembroke, and the beautiful Welsh girl, Nest, daughter of Rhys ap Tewdwr.

Marriage alliances between Welshmen and Anglo-Norman ladies were less frequent. Cadwgan ap Bleddyn married the daughter of the Shropshire marcher lord, Picot de Sai, but she remained in Welsh eyes 'the Frenchwoman who was his wife'. Of her two sons, the elder was given the French name, Henry, and the younger was given the Welsh name, Gruffydd.

At the end of the twelfth century and the beginning of the thirteenth, a change can be discerned. The Lord Rhys married one of his sons, Gruffydd, to Maud, the daughter of the marcher lord, William de Braiose, and in 1198 when the royal officials wished to release Gruffydd from custody, his wife was taken as a hostage for his good behaviour. The king's agents had to hire a small boat to transport her from Bridgenorth to Gloucester. Another marriage with the same family was arranged in the next generation. The northern princes rarely married out of Wales. Dafydd ab Owain married Emma of Anjou at the end of the twelfth century. His nephew Llywelyn the Great (or Fawr) married Joan, natural daughter of King John. It was Llywelyn who, by deliberate policy, sought to strengthen his dynasty by arranging marriage alliances with border families—with Braiose, Lacy, Mortimer, Clifford, and the earl of Chester. Not even the infidelity of his wife Joan, and the summary execution of her paramour, William de Braiose, in 1230 were allowed to interfere with this policy. Certainly, a Welsh prince closely linked with a group of powerful marcher lords was a dangerous man, as Henry III discovered. But this aspect of Norman-Welsh relationships belongs to the thirteenth century, not the twelfth. In the earlier period, mutual hatred and suspicion were partially allayed by comparatively rare marriage alliances between leading families of the two races.

To see how a marcher family could become closely identified with their Welsh lordship, and so with the wider sphere of Welsh social and political life, we can look at the changing fortunes and attitudes of the lords of Brecknock from the conquest of the kingdom by Bernard of Neufmarché in the 1090s to the fall of William de Braiose in 1210. For Bernard himself, his Welsh lands were undoubtedly his greatest acquisition, and compared with Brycheiniog his other possessions in England were of minor significance. When he died, his estates passed to his daughter Sybil and her husband, Miles of Gloucester. This marriage was intended by King Henry I as a reward for the services which Miles and his family had rendered the crown. It also gave the king the opportunity to ensure that a marcher lordship of considerable strategic importance should be in the hands of a man well-disposed towards himself. But Miles already had his own patrimony in England, and the English possessions of his family were increasing steadily. He was deeply involved in the business of royal administration, and all his interests lay in England. He was no stranger in Brecknock, but he may not have known it very well, and there is little sign that he had more than a casual interest in the fortunes of Brecon priory. His son, Roger, also received a wealthy heiress, the daughter of another prominent administrator, Payn fitz John. She brought her husband rich possessions in England and the hope of valuable estates in Herefordshire. Miles and Roger were both men of power and influence. They dominated the local administration of Gloucestershire and, to a lesser extent, Herefordshire.

When Miles became earl of Hereford in 1141 it was clear recognition of where the main interests and hopes of the family lay. (Gloucestershire was the focal point of their activities, but Henry I's son, Robert, already held the title of earl of Gloucester.)

Their Welsh possessions were a valuable adjunct to their English estates. Miles was particularly concerned with the fortunes of the Angevin party in England. He was one of the principal supporters of the Empress Matilda, daughter of Henry I, and from 1139 most of his energies were directed towards securing for her the throne of England. He died in 1143, and the active phase of the civil wars between Matilda and Stephen drew to a close in the late 1140s. By 1149, Matilda had withdrawn from England, and her supporters were left to play a waiting game as Stephen's authority became more firmly and more obviously established in England. Earl Roger had more time to think of his Welsh possessions, and he seems to have spent some time there, living at Brecon castle. He was a generous benefactor of Brecon priory. His career ended in disaster, for in 1155 he was unwise enough to rebel against Henry II, and he paid to the full the price of failure. He retired to the monastery of St. Peter's, Gloucester, and within a matter of months he was dead. Then the cost of failure became crystal clear. The earldom of Hereford was suppressed. His brothers were allowed to retain the hereditary office of constable which had belonged to the family for three generations, but they were not given any power. Walter of Hereford, who succeeded Earl Roger, was gradually squeezed out of the local administration of Gloucestershire and Herefordshire, and he went to the Holy Land, where he died. His younger brothers, Henry and Maihel, succeeded him in turn, and they seem to have withdrawn to their Welsh lordship, and to have retired unobtrusively from the English scene. Henry was killed in a local feud with Seisyll ap Dyfnwal, and Maihel was killed in an accident at Bronllys castle. Earl Miles had acquired the neighbouring lordship of Abergavenny, which passed to his heirs, but they seem to have considered Brecon and Brecknock as their natural refuge, if not their home.

This phase of the family's history had come to an end by 1165, and their possessions were then divided between their sisters. The eldest, Margaret, wife of Humphrey de Bohun, secured most of the English estates once held by her father. She deliberately abandoned his marcher possessions, though, by a curious accident of inheritance, her descendants acquired a share of the lordship of Brecknock again in the thirteenth century, and the Bohuns were to be closely associated with Brecon in the later middle ages. Another sister, Lucy, wife of Herbert fitz Herbert, was excluded from the settlement, and she spent many years before she secured for herself and her successors a part of the lordship of Brecknock. That share came to be known in the thirteenth century as the lordship of Blaenllynfi. The third sister, Bertha, was married to William de Braiose, already lord of Builth and Radnor, and they claimed the honours of Brecknock and Abergavenny as their share of the family inheritance. It looks as if William de Braiose moved the centre of his border interests to Brecon, for he and his successors were closely linked with the castle and lordship. The Braiose family had the habit, common enough among the magnates of northern France, of using the same Christian name in successive generations, and there was rarely a time in the twelfth and early thirteenth centuries when there was not a William de Braiose playing his part in the life of the Welsh Marches.

William de Braiose (son of William and Bertha), who was to become a political figure of the first importance in the reign of John, was much involved in the local intrigues of the March. He determined to avenge the death of Henry of Hereford, and by treachery he persuaded Seisyll ap Dyfnwal and his elder son into Abergavenny castle where they were put to death. He then carried the attack into the countryside, harrying Seisyll's lands, capturing his wife, and killing another son not yet grown to manhood. The *Brut* described the crime in vivid terms:

> And immediately after that, Seisyll ap Dyfnwal was slain through treachery in the castle of Abergavenny by the lord of Brycheiniog. And along with him Geoffrey, his son, and the best men of Gwent were slain. And the French made for Seisyll's court; and after seizing Gwladus, his wife, they slew Cad-

waladr, his son. And on that day there befell a pitiful massacre in Gwent. And from that time forth, after that treachery, none of the Welsh dared place trust in the French.

It was not the only incident of savagery which marked—and indeed marred—William de Braiose's career as a lord of the March. In 1197 there was more violence, as the *Brut* records:

> In that year Trahaearn Fychan of Brycheiniog, a brave eminent man and of gentle lineage, with the niece of the Lord Rhys—his sister's daughter—as his wife, came incautiously to Llangors, to the court of his lord, William de Breos, and there he was seized and imprisoned. And as a pitiful example and with unusual cruelty he was bound by his feet to the tail of a strong horse, and was thus drawn along the streets of Brecon as far as the gallows; and there his head was struck off and he was hanged by his feet; and he was for three days on the gallows, after his brother and his son and his wife, niece of the lord Rhys, had fled from such peril as that.

The savagery was exceptional, though Welshmen had suffered from such high-handed treatment on a number of occasions. In 1179, for example, Cadwallon ap Madog, who had been a hostage of the king, was released by Henry II but was murdered by the men of Roger Mortimer. The king exacted swift justice from Roger and all who had been involved in this crime. It is scarcely to be wondered at that hatred should be a major ingredient in the politics of the March. By chance, the wife and son of William de Braiose themselves had similar ill-fortune when he fell upon evil days. He was a close friend and adviser of King John, and he was one of a very small number of men who could have known the full details of a crime which shocked the magnates of France and England at the beginning of the thirteenth century. John was fighting for the right to rule England and the French possessions of his ancestors, and the leading figure in the opposition was his nephew, Arthur of Brittany, the young heir to John's elder brother, Geoffrey. In 1202 Arthur was taken prisoner, and he disappeared in circumstances which led men to think that he had been murdered. Ugly rumours soon spread that John killed the young prince with his own hands. William de Braiose was one of the few men who might have known the truth, and it seems that he passed on his version of the story to his wife. She, in turn, let it be known that she was well-informed about what had happened. When William de Braiose fell from power, she and her son fell into the king's hands, and they, too, died under suspicious circumstances. It was said that they were starved to death in one of John's castles, probably at Corfe. Savagery was not confined to the Welsh border!

The conflict of loyalties and passions can also be seen in the early Norman settlement of west Wales. Gerald of Windsor married Nest, daughter of Rhys ap Tewdwr, and policy and private action alike were affected. She was abducted in 1109 by Owain ap Cadwgan, who eventually restored her to her outraged husband. Gerald waited long for his revenge, but in 1116 Owain and a band of companions were returning without suspicion after a successful attack in which he had surprised a group of refugees not far from Carmarthen. Owain was working, at this time, in the interests of the English king, and he did not expect the Normans to attack him. But Gerald of Windsor and his men seized their opportunity, and Owain was left dead where he fell. A daughter of Gerald and Nest, Angharad, was married to William of Barry, lord of Manorbier, and the Welsh strain of the fitz Geralds was continued also in the house of Barry. The youngest son of William and Angharad was named Gerald, and to posterity he is best known as Gerald the Welshman. He was unquestionably the most articulate Welshman of the twelfth century, and a prolific writer; from his pen we have many vignettes of Welsh life and of conditions as they were in the Marches. He was intensely proud of his double inheritance. 'I am', he said, 'sprung from the princes of Wales and from the barons of the Marches, and when I see injustice in either race I hate it.' He spent much of his life in the service of the Angevin kings, who obviously found him useful because of his connection with the princes of south Wales. The barons of the March had become deeply involved in a new adventure in the 1170s. It was an attempt to restore the banished king of Leinster, and it led to extensive Norman infiltration in Ireland. For the last thirty years of the twelfth century, Gerald's Norman cousins were playing a major part in these Irish adventures. When, in 1183, Henry II decided to send his youngest son, John, to Ireland, Gerald of Wales was a useful man to send with him. Gerald was also a cleric, and as archdeacon of Brecon and, later, bishop-elect of St. David's, he was a leading figure in an attempt to secure for St. David's the status of an archbishopric. He was a scholar of some note, and was very much at home among fellow-scholars at Paris, or in the small school of theology at Lincoln. In his writings, and especially in his *Description of Wales* and *Itinerary through Wales,* he has provided historians with much valuable material for an understanding of Wales and the Marches in the twelfth century.

Local feuds and disputes were the warp and woof of Welsh life. The Welsh princes and members of the lesser dynasties often produced large families. There were complaints that the Welsh had small regard for the marriage discipline of the Church, and that they made but little distinction between legitimate and illegitimate children. When Owain ap Cadwgan was slain his brothers shared his possessions between them. This is how the *Brut* lists their names:

> Madog, son of Cadwgan by Gwenllian, daughter of Gruffudd ap Cynan; Einion, son of Cadwgan by Sannan, daughter of Dyfnwal; Morgan, son of Cadwgan by Ellylw, daughter of Cedifor ap Gollwyn, the man who had been lord over all Dyfed; Henry, son of Cadwgan by the Frenchwoman his wife, daughter to Picot, a leader of the French; and by her there was another son, his name was Gruffudd; the sixth son was Maredudd by Euron, daughter of Hoeddlyw ap Cadwgan ab Elystan.

To cite another example, Owain Gwynedd had nine sons and daughters. Such families made for both personal and political jealousies. Gerald of Wales saw another facet of this problem.

> Another heavy grievance also prevails (he wrote); the princes entrust the education of their children to the care of the principal men of their country, each of whom, after the death of his father, endeavours, by every possible means, to exalt his own charge above his neighbours. From which cause great disturbances have frequently arisen amongst brothers, and terminated in the most cruel and unjust murders; and on which account friend-

ships are found to be more sincere between foster-brothers, than between those who are connected by the natural ties of brotherhood. It is also remarkable, that brothers show more affection to one another dead, than when living; for they persecute the living even unto death, but revenge the deceased with all their power.

Between 1070 and 1200 the *Brut y Tywysogyon* records the death of over fifty prominent Welshmen who were killed, in this way, by their compatriots. In most cases treachery and guile were essential features of the story; in many cases, brother killed brother, or cousin put cousin to death. There is a small number of instances in which men were less merciful to their enemies, and preferred instead to blind and mutilate their victims.

It is against such a background that we must seek to judge the violence and intrigue which marked the history of the marcher lords of the twelfth century. Welsh prince and Norman lord were each engaged in a quest for power, and few were over-scrupulous as to the means which they employed. The most interesting feature is that they were seeking the same kind of power. A marcher lord differed markedly from other magnates of Norman England. He had more power in his own right. He was less susceptible to royal control. As far as the boundaries of the English kingdom, the Norman and Angevin kings maintained a very real and effective authority. It could best be symbolised at the end of the twelfth century by the extent to which men of all degrees in society could be brought to justice in the king's court. A later age would use the phrase, 'the king's writ did not run in the March', and the meaning, though technical, is basically very simple. The king could not give direct instructions and be sure that they would be carried out; he could not use royal officials to ensure that this will was obeyed. The marcher lords had, therefore, a measure of freedom which was quite untypical of medieval England. They were not entirely removed from the king's control. Many of them held lands in England, and could be answerable to the king as his tenants-in-chief there. Throughout the twelfth century, successive English kings tried to exert a direct influence over the Marches, and occasionally over Wales itself. William the Conqueror had visited St. David's as early as 1081. His journey could be taken as a pilgrimage to a venerable shrine, or as a show of force, designed to impress Rhys ap Tewdwr in particular. Perhaps the Conqueror had more than one motive when he planned and made the long journey to the west coast. William Rufus and Henry I each attempted large-scale attacks in Wales; so, too, did Henry II, though his campaigns in Wales were very undistinguished. The north was not materially affected, and in the south he achieved far greater success by making Rhys ap Gruffydd a willing ally rather than an unwilling vassal. John was himself a marcher lord, and he intervened directly in marcher affairs. It was also possible for the king to ensure that the right man was available in the Marches. Henry I used appointments to marcher lordships as a convenient way of influencing events in Wales. The Clares in Ceredigion and Miles of Gloucester in Brecknock are the most obvious examples. Later in the twelfth century, William Marshal and William de Braiose were given extensive, if unofficial, powers and were allowed to dominate the March; while in the next generation, Hubert de Burgh played a similar role.

Behind all these forms of intervention there was the reality, unpleasant as it might be for the crown, that the marcher lords claimed and exercised a freedom of action in dealing with their lordships in Wales. The explanation which has now been firmly established is that each was exercising the rights of a prince in his own lordship. The Normans were great adaptors. They were usually in a small minority wherever they settled, and adaptation and adjustment were a major part of their success in holding down their conquests. In England they found a society in which the powers of a centralised kingship had long been recognised. The king's will could be transmitted to royal officials, and these officials could impose it upon local communities. This concept of power they accepted and strengthened. In Wales they found a land of many princes, with each dynasty claiming and exercising regalian rights. The right of plunder, or perhaps it should be described as a right to wage war, was one which they saw in use often and again. As they took over Welsh

77

lands and converted them into lordships, so they took over the rights which the Welsh rulers whom they displaced had once exercised. There may be a danger that this view will be interpreted in a narrowly constitutional or legal sense, when it is doubtful if the Normans saw it or understood it with such precision. But it does seem clear that financial and legal rights were claimed on this basis and developed as the middle ages progressed, and it is clear, too, that the marcher lords wanted to use their right of war and plunder as they could see their Welsh neighbours using it. In that sense, the arrival of the Norman lords of the March was an extension of the traditional pattern of life in Wales: the country remained a place in which many princes claimed royal powers, and in which marcher lords claimed the same kind of powers wherever they secured a permanent hold. One interesting feature of this is that in Morgannwg the exercise of such powers was not limited to the lord of Glamorgan alone; it was exercised by a number of the magnates holding lordships within the limits of the ancient Welsh kingdom.

In his *Description of Wales* Gerald set out to analyse how the Normans could hope to conquer Wales, and, then, how the Welsh could hope to withstand their attacks. To do so, he had to concentrate on the weaker aspects of both races, but it remains an illuminating piece of writing. He could see that only by a sustained campaign could Wales be conquered, for the Welsh were not equipped by nature or by training for long drawn out resistance.

> Anyone who wished to conquer Wales must be determined to apply a diligent and constant attention to this purpose for one year at least; for a people who with a collected force will not openly attack the enemy in the field, nor wait to be besieged in castles, is not to be overcome at the first onset, but be worn out by prudent delay and patience. Let him divide their strength, and by bribes and promises endeavour to stir up one against another, knowing the spirit of hatred and envy which generally prevails amongst them; and in the autumn let not only the marches, but also the interior part of the country be strongly fortified with castles, provisions, and families which can be trusted. In the meantime, the purchase of corn, cloth and salt,

with which they are usually supplied from England, should be strictly interdicted, to prevent their importation of these articles. from Ireland or the Severn sea, and to facilitate the supply of his own army.

Such plans were a heavy demand to make. John might plan on a big scale to regain his lost French possessions, but no king of England in the twelfth century had resources on this scale. In fact, Gerald was not yet finished.

> Afterwards (he went on), when the severity of winter approaches, when the trees are void of leaves, and the mountains no longer afford pasturage — when they are deprived of any hopes of plunder, and harassed on every side by the repeated attacks of the enemy—let a body of light-armed infantry penetrate into their woody and mountainous retreats, and let these troops be supported and relieved by others; and thus, by frequent changes, and replacing the men who are either fatigued or slain in battle, this nation may be ultimately subdued.

It seemed to Gerald that one thing remained as an essential requirement, and that was that the men of the March should have the chief place in the enterprise.

> In this (he said), as well as in every other military expedition, either in Ireland or in Wales, the natives of the marches, from the constant state of warfare in which they are engaged, and whose manners are formed from the habits of war, are bold and active, skilful on horseback, quick on foot, not nice as to their diet, and ever prepared when necessity requires to abstain both from corn and wine. By such men were the first hostile attacks made upon Wales as well as Ireland, and by such men alone can their final conquest be accomplished.

Despite his education and his urbanity, his experience of the king's court, of the schools of Paris, or of the papal court (or curia) at Rome, Gerald was a frontiersman, and the cult of the frontier was part of his make-up. To subdue Wales would be one thing. To hold it would require constant vigilance, a regular inspection of arms and supplies, a permanent state of readiness all along the borders of Gloucestershire, Herefordshire, Shropshire and Cheshire. Oversight should be 'committed to a man of firm and determined mind; who, during the time of peace, by paying due obedience to the laws, and respect to the government, may render it firm and stable'.

Gerald was, as he said, 'equally connected by birth with each nation', and that prompted him to argue the means by which the Welsh could resist all attempts at conquest.

> If the Welsh were more commonly accustomed to the Gallic mode of arming and depended more on steady fighting than on their agility; if their princes were unanimous and inseparable in their defence; or rather, if they had only one prince, and that a good one; this nation, situated in so powerful, strong, and inaccessible a country, could hardly ever be completely overcome.

The weakness of Gerald's case is that, although there was more in this vein, the hard streak of common sense which underlies his analysis of the conditions which might make for conquest gives way to something approaching sentimentality. He cannot overcome the basic flaw in the political condition of Wales, which, at the risk of repetition, he could summarise under three headings.

> There are three things which ruin this nation, and prevent its enjoying the satisfaction of a fruitful progeny. First, because both the natural and legitimate sons endeavour to divide the paternal inheritance amongst themselves; from which cause, as we have before observed, continual fratricides take place. Secondly, because the education of their sons is committed to the care of the high-born people of the country, who on the death of their fathers, endeavour by all possible means to exalt their pupil; from whence arise murders, conflagrations, and almost a total destruction of the country. And, thirdly, because from the pride and obstinacy of their disposition, they will not (like other nations) subject themselves to the dominion of one lord and king.

Conquest required resources on a massive scale, persistence, and a determined will. Freedom from conquest, on the other hand, required more; it called for the rejection of deep-seated

PLATE 4
Cardiff Castle

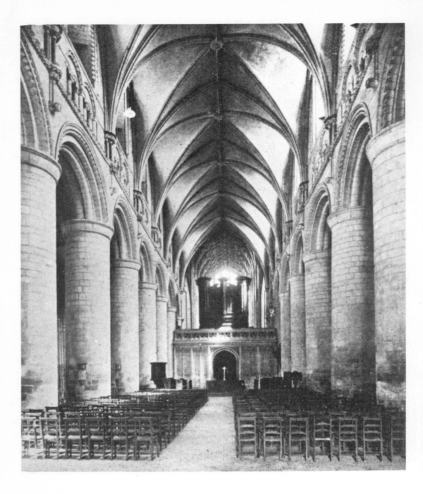

PLATE 5
Norman nave of St. Peter's Abbey, Gloucester,
now Gloucester Cathedral

Welsh traditions, and the substitution of alien ways. What was true in the twelfth century was still true in the last phase of the struggle for survival and independence at the end of the thirteenth century.

Marriage alliances might have been a means of bringing Welsh and Norman together, though Gerald of Wales, with his pride in the fact that he belonged to two races, is exceptional rather than typical of border society. Identification with the affairs of their lordships, which was characteristic of a number of marcher families, might also have contributed to a distinctive marcher society. In fact, as Gerald could see clearly, there were long-term factors at work, and in Wales they made for disunity and disruption. The introduction of Norman settlers deepened the divisions in Welsh society, and added another factor — the question of race — to the problem. If war was a permanent feature of the March, it was not the creation of the frontier, nor of the frontiersman. It was already, and it continued to be, the normal condition of life in medieval Wales.

Chapter Six

The Normans and the Welsh Church

As he tried to assess the career of Robert of Rhuddlan, Orderic
Vitalis had to consider the merciless way in which Robert had
dealt with the Welsh, and he met with what seemed to be an in-
superable difficulty. Like Robert himself, the Welsh were
Christians. 'It is not right,' Orderic declared, 'that Christians
should so oppress their brothers who have been reborn in the
faith of Christ by holy baptism.' Orderic was a monk, with the
simplicity of outlook which was often the product of the clois-
ter. Nevertheless, he had picked out an important element in the
story of the Norman advance. Wales was a Christian land, and
the Church had long been established within her confines. Indeed, without the Welsh Church the story of Christian expansion in the British Isles in the Dark Ages would have been very
different. In general, the Church might be expected to be a civil-
ising, and therefore a softening, influence. The Normans dis-
played little sympathy with the church which they found when
they came to Wales, and to a large extent they refashioned and
remade it during the late eleventh and early twelfth centuries.
Conflict over religion was added to conflict in so many other
spheres of life in Wales. Why should this be?

The Normans were deeply religious. The most violent of
them could swing from treachery and murder to piety and fervour, which were certainly not assumed, and the history of the
Norman baronage in Normandy and in England is full of
sudden conversions. Magnates would choose to die in a monastery, in the habit of a monk or canon. Knights would abandon

the world for a monastic vocation and a life of discipline and asceticism. Increasingly, after Pope Urban II proclaimed the first crusade in 1095, the aristocracy and knightly classes of Europe, and especially of northern France, found an outlet for their professional skills and religious fervour in the Holy Land. Violent conversions were often brought about through fear of the consequences of evil deeds. It is no accident that in those churches where, through sculpture or wall-paintings, artists had attempted to drive home basic religious teaching, the emphasis was on the pains of hell, the punishment of the damned, and the rewards and bliss which awaited the faithful. There were many ways of making recompense for past sins and, if possible, avoiding the terrors of hell, and the most popular was to endow a religious house with gifts of land, with revenue, churches, or valuable rights and privileges. The donor could then become a beneficiary of the prayers of the monks. Observers from a different age, often taking a rather cynical view, may find in all this a measure of insurance against future uncertainties, but it would be doing a grave injustice to the men of the twelfth century not to take seriously the outlook of their age and the sincerity which it could so often produce, naive though it might have been.

The Normans who invaded England followed this practice of endowing religious foundations on a large scale. Many of them were already associated with monasteries in Normandy, and their first instinct was to make generous gifts of English estates and English churches to Norman abbeys. William fitz Osbern had founded two Norman monastic houses in which he was particularly interested, at Lire and Cormeilles, and he made a number of grants to them in England and along the Welsh border. Wihenoc of Monmouth was a Breton who had been established at Monmouth by 1086, and he was a benefactor of the abbey of St. Florent at Saumur, on the Loire. Robert of Rhuddlan and his family were benefactors of the Norman abbey of St. Evroul.

By 1066 there were in England some thirty-five Benedictine monasteries, exactly similar in their way of life, their outward appearance and their organisation to the monasteries of Normandy, and it was not long before the new Norman aristocracy of England began to make gifts to these houses. Before the end of the Conqueror's reign, Norman abbots had been appointed to English monasteries throughout the country, and it was a matter of immediate concern for them to attract new gifts and new sources of income to their houses. At Gloucester, to take one example, there was a Benedictine monastery which had been refounded in 1058 and which was surviving precariously when the Normans invaded England. In 1072 a new abbot, a Norman, Serlo, was appointed, and he completely transformed the abbey, attracting new recruits in large numbers, establishing a rule of life which was notable for its rigour, and beginning the long-term project of building a new monastic church (see plate 5). The list of donors who gave lands and churches to St. Peter's, Gloucester, included Bernard of Neufmarché, the widow of Walter de Lacy, Robert fitz Hamo, members of the family of Miles of Gloucester, Robert, earl of Gloucester, William, earl of Gloucester, William and Maurice of London, and many others associated with the Norman advance into Wales. So it happened that a secondary feature of the Norman conquest of England was the enrichment of a number of old-established English abbeys.

Before long, a third line of development could be seen. William the Conqueror established a new abbey at the site of the battle of Hastings and called it Battle abbey. Roger of Montgomery built the abbey church of St. Peter at Shrewsbury; Hugh of Avranches built the monastery of St. Werburgh at Chester. Lesser families were doing the same, and the rate of expansion of monastic houses in England and along the Marches increased rapidly as the twelfth century advanced. To take two examples: the Lacy family was especially interested in the priory of St. Guthlac's, Hereford, which became a daughter house of St. Peter's, Gloucester; their neighbour, Harold of Ewyas, provided the endowment for another priory at Ewyas, and after many delays this too was established as a cell of St. Peter's, Gloucester. By 1100 there were seventy major Benedictine houses in England. The next hundred years would see the establishment of new monastic orders, like the Cistercian order, the military orders of the Temple and the Hospital, and a number of orders for canons, and abbeys and priories were founded in England on a large scale.

The secular church in Anglo-Saxon England was also organised on lines entirely familiar to the Normans, and the Normans preserved what they found. William I appointed Lanfranc as archbishop of Canterbury in 1070, and the diocesan structure of England was strengthened, synods were held regularly, and something of the ferment which was growing in Europe through the activities of the reforming popes of the mid-eleventh century was transmitted to the English Church.

In Wales the story is dramatically different. As in England, Norman adventurers thought first of monasteries with which they were already closely associated. In the earliest phases of conquest that implied monasteries in northern France such as those enriched by William fitz Osbern or Robert of Rhuddlan. In later phases of the Norman settlement, however, it implied monasteries in England. St. Peter's, Gloucester, did remarkably well, with possessions in Brecknock and Cardigan, in Gwynllŵg and Glamorgan. The munificence of the family of London in the western part of Glamorgan resulted in the foundation of a dependent priory at Ewenny, where a fine Romanesque church was built for the use of the monks. Robert fitz Hamo was founder of Tewkesbury abbey and a most generous benefactor, and this Gloucestershire house also acquired rich possessions in south Wales. Bernard of Neufmarché was obviously impressed with the Conqueror's foundation of Battle abbey, on the site of the battle which had ensured his success. We do not know how the connection came about, but Bernard had in his entourage two monks from Battle, and he was persuaded to hand over to Battle as a dependent priory the church of St. John the Evangelist which he had built beyond the defences of his castle at Brecon. A priory at Carmarthen was another daughter house of Battle abbey.

Such grants were in keeping with what had happened immediately after the Norman conquest of England, but there the parallel ends. There were in Wales no recognisable monastic foundations of the European type. So, there was little hope that

Norman generosity might be transferred to local monasteries. What existed in Wales was the *clas* church, that characteristic Celtic community, which showed little affinity with Benedictine monasticism, and which had more in common with the organised life of secular canons which was to be widespread in Europe in the twelfth century.

Many Benedictine monasteries were established in Wales, usually near the castle, and often in the small borough which developed outside the castle. The priory churches at Abergavenny, Brecon, Kidwelly and Cardigan stand as examples. In Welsh eyes they were alien institutions, taking the place of the *clas* church and attracting wealth which seemed to be little more than the spoils of conquest. What else could be assumed, when Roger, earl of Hereford, promised the monks of Brecon the tithes of all his conquests in Wales? These Benedictine houses rarely gained a hold on Welsh loyalties. Many modern writers consider them to have been agencies of conquest and suppression. It is worth remembering, however, that Benedictine monasticism in the eleventh and twelfth centuries was essentially an urban phenomenon. Only with the new ideas of the Cistercian order would there come once again the sense that a monastery should be established remote from the places where men lived and, for a while at least, free from the influences which town, castle, or court might exert.

The secular church seemed equally strange and unfamiliar. In Wales, the territorial diocese, with its boundaries clearly defined, was virtually unknown. A grouping of Teilo churches or Dewi churches indicated clearly where the interests of one bishop gave way to another, and in eastern parts of Wales, notably in Gwent and Gwynllŵg, there may have been a clearer concept of the diocese as a territorial unit. In English dioceses like Chichester, or Worcester, or even in a border diocese like Hereford, the Normans could see what were the limits of the bishopric, and what was the range of authority of its bishop. In St. David's, as elsewhere in Wales, they could not define the limits in such clear terms. There was the added problem that they did not establish firm control over all the Welsh bishoprics. A bishopric which covered Glamorgan was in their hands early in the twelfth century. In the diocese of St. David's, Norman invaders were a grave problem for the bishop, taking lands over which he had authority, so that by 1115 the bishopric was dominated by Norman magnates, some of whom pillaged the estates of his church. Bangor was held briefly at the end of the eleventh century, and although the bishopric at Llanelwy, later to be called St. Asaph, was firmly under Norman influence, its history is puzzling and enigmatic in the extreme.

The Welsh bishoprics were gradually transformed. They became territorial units with clearly defined boundaries within which the bishop exercised his jurisdiction. This was only achieved with great difficulty, and there was conflict between the bishop of Llandaff and his neighbours, the bishops of St. David's and Hereford, before the diocesan boundaries of Llandaff could be fixed beyond dispute. In a celebrated case, the bishop of St. Asaph tried to reconsecrate the church of Ceri, right on the boundaries of his own diocese and St. David's. He was forestalled by the resourceful archdeacon of Brecon, Gerald of Wales, who refused to allow the church of Ceri to be included within the diocese of St. Asaph. A type of diocesan organisation familiar in Europe was encouraged in Wales, with archdeacons and rural deans having clearly defined jurisdictions, and with each playing a formal part in the administration of the diocese. It was not without importance that the Welsh bishops of the twelfth century attracted to their service a number of able clerics trained in the 'schools', those institutions of advanced education which, by the early thirteenth century, would be called universities. In common with bishops throughout western Europe, the Welsh diocesans were able to make good use of such men. Happily, documents dealing with a wide range of ecclesiastical business have survived from all the Welsh sees, and the story of the development of the Welsh Church during the age of Norman expansion can be written with some confidence.

The early advance of the Normans from Chester led to the appointment of a Breton, Hervé, as bishop of Bangor in 1092. He was a member of the Conqueror's court, and a man of some influence. In the revival of Welsh vigour from 1094 onwards, he was driven from his cathedral church of St. Deiniol, and for some years he complained of the savage treatment he had received from the 'barbarians' who controlled his see. He was eventually allowed to hold the abbey of Ely in Cambridgeshire, and when Henry I created a new bishopric of Ely in 1107, Hervé became the first bishop of that diocese. It was 1120 before another bishop was consecrated to Bangor. What is difficult to explain is that the bishopric of St. Asaph was not filled until 1143, some seventy years after the Normans first swept into Rhos and Rhufoniog.

In the south, the traditions of St. David's as an episcopal centre were very strong and they were maintained with dignity and vigour by a succession of Welsh bishops in the eleventh century: Bleddud, Sulien, the distinguished scholar-bishop, and Abraham. The last in this succession was Wilfrid, who became bishop in 1085 and died in 1115. Wilfrid watched as the Normans attacked and invaded until they controlled much of his diocese. He was followed by the first bishop of St. David's to be appointed by the Normans, Bernard, the queen's chancellor, who guided the affairs of the diocese from 1115 to 1148.

Llandaff presents some of the most intriguing and baffling problems connected with the Welsh Church in the twelfth century. The first impact of Norman infiltration in Gwent and Morgannwg occurred during the episcopate of Bishop Herewald, who died in 1104 and was succeeded three years later by Bishop Urban. The immediate problem is to know when the diocese of Llandaff was founded. Llandaff was a useful centre, not too far from the castle and borough of Cardiff; but the main centre of ecclesiastical activity in Morgannwg was the famous *clas* church at Llancarfan. Its members (or *claswyr*) were a powerful clan, and in the twelfth century they were closely associated with the cathedral church at Llandaff. If the evidence of the *Book of Llandaff* is taken at face value, the diocese could claim to have an ancient origin, but that would not be an easy thesis to defend. It has been suggested that the territorial diocese of Llandaff was a Norman creation, and that the *claswyr* of Llancarfan, by making common cause with their new Norman lords, carried their old influence from Llancarfan

to Llandaff. It is a plausible theory. Much turns on the inter-
pretation of the *Book of Llandaff,* which purports to contain
material relating to the history of the diocese from the sixth century onwards. As it now is, the *Book* was clearly 'edited' in the
twelfth century, during the episcopate of Bishop Urban, and it
is a matter of dispute as to how much editorial work was
actually done. Should it be called a forgery, or was this editing
merely a process, however extensive, of adding new material to
old texts? That there is a core of genuine old material, some of it
dating back to the sixth century, cannot be doubted, but much
has been added to it. Then, it is apparent that there were
bishops exercising authority in the eastern areas of Gwent and
Gwynllŵg, and in that disputed territory of Erging which, by
the twelfth century, had been firmly incorporated into Herefordshire. Little is known about them, but it may be that they,
too, had some share in the establishment of the cathedral at
Llandaff. So, an alternative suggestion about the foundation of
the diocese is that it should be dated somewhere in the eleventh
century, and that it may be connected especially with a bishop
called Joseph. These problems have occasioned some of the
most brilliant research at present in progress in Welsh ecclesiastical history, but many of the answers are still no more than
tentative.

The critical question which caused such heart-searching in
Wales in the twelfth century was that of authority: by whom
were Welsh bishops to be appointed, and to whom did they owe
obedience? On the one hand, the settlement of the Investiture
Contest as far as it affected England had left the king with the
major influence in the choice of new bishops and abbots, and
they were required to pay homage to the king before their
consecration. On the other hand, the claims which had been
made so boldly for Canterbury by Archbishop Lanfranc were
maintained. New bishops, including those appointed to Welsh
sees, were consecrated by the archbishop of Canterbury and, as
a matter of course, they made an oath of obedience to him. The
Welsh bishoprics were brought firmly into the province of
Canterbury, not by any declaration of policy, but rather by the
quiet, effective process of administrative procedure. The

political advantages of this were obvious, and the princes of north Wales were determined to break the control of Canterbury over the northern sees. But no-one was more active or determined than Bernard, the first Norman bishop of St. David's, to secure the independence of his see, and its recognition as an archbishopric for Wales. He failed, though he might well have succeeded, for there was much discussion about the centres of authority in the church during the 1140s, and only a few years after his death, in 1152, the papacy freed the Irish Church from the domination of Canterbury and created four metropolitan archbishoprics in Ireland. It would be a sad misreading of events to think of the fight for the independence of St. David's as one of the unattainable aims of twelfth-century politics. As it was, Bernard's determined struggle was a major factor contributing to the strength of the case which a later champion of St. David's, Gerald of Wales, would put forward at the end of the twelfth century.

First of all, there were problems of definition to be solved, and Bernard of St. David's and Urban of Llandaff were both active in their determination to win the advantage in a struggle for the recognition of the boundaries of their dioceses. The *Book of Llandaff* was drawn up in its present form as evidence in this dispute, and there is no doubt that the material which it contains was edited carefully, and where necessary much amended, in order to make it the more convincing. The interesting thing is that these bishops chose to use the pope as arbiter in their dispute, and Urban was indefatigable in travelling to Rome in order to plead his case. The papacy did not need to impose its authority over the Welsh Church, for Urban and Bernard found it useful to invoke, and therefore to recognise, papal authority.

Bishop Bernard tried hard but unsuccessfully to obtain from Pope Eugenius III acknowledgement that St. David's was the metropolitan church of Wales. Himself an alien, Bernard took up a case which only those with long understanding of the history of St. David's could have put together. His fight was taken up again at the end of the twelfth century by Gerald of Wales, a fierce partisan of the rights of St. David's. From 1198 until

1203, Gerald was bishop-elect of St. David's. It was the great ambition of his life to be bishop of the premier see in Wales, but he was destined to be disappointed, for he was never consecrated. His election was disputed, and he had to fight his cause at the papal court in the presence of Pope Innocent III. He also fought brilliantly for the recognition of St. David's as a metropolitan see. He had powerful enemies, none more determined or more influential than Hubert Walter, archbishop of Canterbury, papal legate, and a leading figure in the king's administration, first as justiciar and later as chancellor. By 1203, Gerald was forced to accept defeat, and Wales remained part of the province of Canterbury, as it was to be until 1920. Wales defied all the efforts of the Norman and Angevin kings to impose any sense of unity upon the land. Where the strongest of the English kings of the twelfth century failed, the archbishops of Canterbury succeeded, and their success, binding Welsh churchmen in allegiance to themselves, was to be an important influence from which the English crown derived considerable benefit.

The gradual creation of a normal diocesan administration meant that the bishop and his agents could have more effective oversight of the church. At a local level, as Gerald of Wales often complained, the church was bedevilled by hereditary succession. 'Married' clergy ignored the rigours of canon law, and son succeeded father in the family benefice. Gerald also disliked the large number of clerics who could claim some share in the parish church, for there were as many of these portionaries as there were influential men in the parish. The abuse long outlived Gerald himself. Early in the thirteenth century at Llowes, there were three portionaries, and when the parish priest of Glasbury wished to check their claims, which he regarded as pretentious, he had to be content that as each of them died his share of Llowes should pass into his control. As archdeacon of Brecon, Gerald was a reformer, anxious to bring order and decency where he found laxity and family influence (or nepotism). The same evil existed also in the higher echelons of the church, but there Gerald was more reluctant to condemn it. His uncle, David fitz Gerald, bishop of St. David's, gave him the archdeaconry of Brecon, and when he himself was an old man he took care to hand the office to a nephew, thereby keeping it in the family.

Efficient and stern administration could not make up for the loss of identification between Welsh church and Welsh people. Gerald knew that from his own experience. When he was engaged in the struggle for the independence of St. David's, he offered to withdraw as bishop-elect if the king would nominate a suitable candidate. His definition of such a man was that he should acknowledge the customs of both peoples, Norman and Welsh, and should devote himself to his pastoral duties as bishop. The barrier created by a new type of monasticism, an unfamiliar diocesan structure, and a church patently identified with the invaders, was reinforced by a conflict of language. French and Latin were the languages normally in use, and Welsh, which was the usual channel of expression for the vast majority of people in Wales, was little used. In 1188, Baldwin, archbishop of Canterbury, travelled around Wales and preached the cause of the third crusade. Sermons exhorting faithful Christian men to take the Cross and to fight for the defence of the Holy Land were preached in towns and in large churches throughout Wales, but they were preached in either Latin or French. Gerald himself did some of the preaching and, as he tells us, made a great impression on all who heard him, but he, too, used these alien tongues. Alexander, archdeacon of Bangor, travelled with the archbishop and his party to translate all these exhortations into Welsh.

Two things made a marked difference. One was that the northern bishoprics came under the influence of the rulers of Gwynedd and Powys. Gruffydd ap Cynan secured the consecration of David the Scot as bishop of Bangor in 1120, and David is believed to have been a Welshman. In 1139, Maurice (or Meurig) was appointed to Bangor, and once again the influence of the prince of Gwynedd was strong. This time the prince was Owain Gwynedd, and it is not clear whether he and his brother, Cadwaladr, took the initiative and were directly responsible for Meurig's appointment, or whether they merely gave their approval to a name proposed by the English king.

Meurig had to deal with Henry II and he gave fealty to the English king, a step which caused resentment and controversy in Wales. There followed a long vacancy from 1161 to 1177 before the next bishop of Bangor was consecrated, and again he was a Welshman, Gwion. During this vacancy there were protracted disputes with the king of England, on the one hand, and with the archbishop of Canterbury, on the other, as Owain tried to establish that Bangor was independent of their control. He could speak and write of 'his' bishopric and 'his' bishop in terms exactly parallel to those which Henry II could use in any part of his dominions. At the end of the century, a Welsh candidate, Roland, was twice passed over as bishop, but Llywelyn ab Iorwerth established cordial relationships with the English nominee who was elected in 1197, Robert of Shrewsbury.

St. Asaph was not filled until 1143, and for the next thirty years the position of the bishop was uncertain in the extreme. One bishop, Godfrey, solved the problems of poverty and remoteness by forging close links with the wealthy abbey of St. Albans. He was under heavy pressure to return to his diocese and become an active bishop, or else to resign, and in 1175 he was finally brought to the point of resignation. Gerald of Wales presumably had him especially in mind when he wrote of those English bishops in Wales who could be found begging at abbeys in England, pleading for more money at the king's Exchequer, asking for translation to more lucrative sees, or seeking to have their present incomes augmented — and, as he averred, acting as spies between England and Wales, and generally neglecting their pastoral duties! Despite the uncertain state of affairs at St. Asaph, and the fluctuations which can be seen at Bangor, the foundations were laid for that close accord which existed between the northern bishops and the princes of Wales in the thirteenth century.

The second change which introduced a new element into the Welsh ecclesiastical scene was the appearance of the Cistercian monks in Wales. The Cistercians, so called from their first monastery at Cîteux, were anxious for stricter discipline and fewer social and economic encumbrances. Monasteries which were Cistercian, or which belonged to similar reforming movements like those associated with the abbeys of Tiron or Savigny, were founded in the area dominated by the marcher lords, and they therefore remained Anglo-Norman in outlook and loyalty. Houses like Tintern, Margam and Neath acquired large tracts of hill country and grazing rights, even from Welsh donors. They were scarely to be distinguished from other Cistercian houses founded in England. In 1140, however, a group of Cistercian monks from Clairvaux settled at Whitland, and in the course of time a number of colonies were sent out into mid-Wales and north Wales. Cwmhir was founded in 1143, Strata Florida in 1164, Strata Marcella in 1170, and each of these later founded daughter houses at Cymer, Caerleon, Aberconwy, and Valle Crucis.

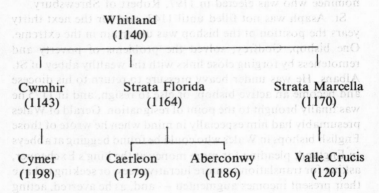

	Whitland	
	(1140)	
Cwmhir	Strata Florida	Strata Marcella
(1143)	(1164)	(1170)
Cymer	Caerleon Aberconwy	Valle Crucis
(1198)	(1179) (1186)	(1201)

These later abbeys became closely associated with Welsh ruling dynasties and attracted Welsh recruits. They were remote from Anglo-Norman influence and were identified with Welsh loyalties. Drawing upon their records, the *Brut y Tywysogyon* was compiled at the end of the thirteenth century.

The story of the Welsh Church in the Norman period is one of the intrusion of new men and new ideas into a Welsh setting. The old Welsh *clas* church was submerged, and the new institutions were especially linked with the invaders and with the castles which were the symbols of their dominance. Yet, whatever their birth and their allegiance, men like Bernard of

St. David's and Urban of Llandaff could seek to build a strong and independent church in Wales. As in the secular sphere, it could not be said that the new ecclesiastical pattern imposed on Wales was likely to destroy traditions of independence.

Chapter Seven

Conclusion

In one sense, the Norman conquerors imposed on Wales a patchwork of political and social units. Independent lordships were created in which Norman domination was assured by a small minority, a military élite, while at the same time varying social patterns were created within each lordship. In another sense, the Norman settlement created a stalemate. Full-scale conquest was beyond the limits of even the most powerful lords of the March. The kings of England made a number of attempts to impose their authority over Wales, but by the end of the twelfth century none had devoted to the task the time or the resources which were necessary for complete conquest.

It would be easy to distort the picture and to suggest that one race more than the other had a monopoly of virtue or of vice. Each tended to despise and disparage the other, and even their friends could not easily hide the weaknesses of character which so often were allowed to become dominant. The writer of the *Brut,* recording clashes between Welsh and Norman, was happy to note that 'the French, according to their custom, fled and some of them were captured, others were slain'. The same writer attributed to King Henry I the question, 'Do you know that accursed petty thief Gruffudd ap Rhys, who is molesting my magnates?' Yet there were times when other assessments could creep in. As the Welsh recognised, a defeat could be due to Norman efficiency, 'as it is the way with the French to do everything with diligence and circumspection'. Gerald of Wales noticed with regret that

> In war this nation the Welsh is very severe in the first attack,
> terrible by their clamour and looks, filling the air with horrid
> shouts and the deep-toned clangour of very long trumpets; swift
> and rapid in their advances and frequent throwing of darts. Bold
> in the first onset, they cannot bear a repulse, being easily thrown
> into confusion as soon as they turn their backs; and they trust to
> flight for safety, without attempting to rally.

Perhaps the truth is that Normans and Welsh were closer to
each other in many respects than they realised. If they did not
make congenial neighbours, they were men who adopted
similar standards in their dealings with their fellows. In a
famous passage, Gerald painted in most cruel terms the darker
side of the Welsh character.

> These people are no less light in mind than in body, and are by
> no means to be relied upon. They are easily urged to undertake
> any action, and are as easily checked from prosecuting it — a
> people quick in action, but more stubborn in a bad than in a
> good cause, and constant only in acts of inconstancy. They pay
> no respect to oaths, faith, or truth; and so lightly do they esteem
> the covenant of faith, held so inviolable by other nations, that it
> is usual to sacrifice their faith for nothing, by holding forth the
> right hand, not only in serious and important concerns, but even
> on every trifling occasion, and for the confirmation of almost
> every common assertion. They never scruple at taking a false
> oath for the sake of any temporary emolument or advantage; so
> that in civil and ecclesiastical causes, each party, being ready to
> swear whatever seems expedient to its purpose, endeavours to
> prove and defend, although the venerable laws, by which oaths
> are deemed sacred, and truth is honoured and respected, by
> favouring the accused and throwing odium upon the accuser,
> impose the burden of bringing proofs upon the latter. But to a
> people so cunning and crafty, this yoke is pleasant, and this
> burden is light.

A chronicler, writing a century earlier in Italy, Geoffrey
Malaterra, summed up the characteristics of the Normans as he
saw them in that very different part of Europe. His account is as
revealing and as searching as anything Gerald could say.

> The Normans are a cunning and revengeful people; eloquence
> and dissimulation appear to be their hereditary qualities; they
> can stoop to flatter; but unless they are curbed by the restraint of

law they indulge the licentiousness of nature and passion. Their princes affect the praise of popular munificence; the people blend the extremes of avarice and prodigality, and in their eager thirst of wealth and dominion, they despise whatever they possess and hope whatever they desire. Arms and horses, the luxury of dress, the exercise of hunting and hawking, are the delight of the Normans; but on pressing occasions they can endure with incredible patience the inclemency of every climate and the toil and abstinence of a military life.

Put men of these characteristics, Welsh and Norman, in conflict, and the story which ensues is scarcely likely to be edifying, nor one marked by high ideals and clear statesmanship. There was much villainy, and much heroism; there was, inevitably, much suffering, particularly for those who did not have the enjoyment of battle and conquest. But all this is characteristic of a frontier in any era. The important issue always is to know what will grow out of frontier conditions in a more settled age? That, in Wales, was a question to which no answer was given at any time during the twelfth century.

Suggestions for further reading

A. *Sources*

The main Welsh source is the *Brut y Tywysogyon* (or *The Chronicle of the Princes)*. It was originally a Latin chronicle drawn up in the late thirteenth century, and it is known in two Welsh translations which were made independently in different Welsh monasteries. They are identified from two famous manuscripts: Peniarth Ms. 20 at the National Library of Wales, and the 'Red Book of Hergest' at Jesus College, Oxford. Closely associated with the *Brut* is the *Brenhinedd y Saeson* (or *The Kings of the Saxons)*, which is a conflation of the *Brut* and a series of annals from an English monastery. The *Brut* is based on earlier materials, some of which have survived; the most important is the *Annales Cambriae*. The *Brut y Tywysogyon* and the *Brenhinedd y Saeson* are now available in a splendid series of volumes edited, with English translations, by Thomas Jones (Cardiff, 1952-1971).

There is a considerable amount of information about Wales in English sources; a good selection of sources relating to England between 1042 and 1189 has been published in *English Historical Documents, ii, 1042-1189,* edited by David C. Douglas and G. W. Greenway (London, 1953), and for the period 1189-1327 in *English Historical Documents, iii, 1189-1327,* edited by H. Rothwell (London, 1975). A useful discussion of Welsh historical sources is available in *Medieval Wales*, by R. Ian Jack (London, 1972).

Two twelfth-century historians have much to tell us about Wales and the Marches. One is Orderic Vitalis, whose *Ecclesiastical History* is a survey of the achievements of the Normans in Europe. It is now being published in a new edition, with English translation, by Marjorie Chibnall (Oxford Medieval Texts Series: Volumes II (1969), III (1972), and IV (1973) have so far appeared). The other is Gerald of Wales, who wrote so vividly about Wales and includes valuable material about Wales, the Welsh Church, and Welsh personalities in many of his works. His two books, the *Itinerary through Wales* and the *Description of Wales,* form the best introduction to the writer and his style. These are readily available in translation (Everyman's Library, first published in 1908).

The cartularies of many English monasteries, especially those along the border, contain valuable material. Much of this is available in calendar form in *Episcopal Acts Relating to Welsh Dioceses, 1066-1272.* The first two volumes were published in 1946 and 1948 for the Historical Society of the Church in Wales, edited by J. Conway Davies. They include an introduction which deals with the whole of Wales, and texts in English for the two southern dioceses of St. David's and Llandaff. A third volume dealing with Bangor and St. Asaph is in preparation.

B. *Secondary Works*

The list which follows is confined mainly to recent books, and to a very small selection of articles. Full bibliographies of the Norman period are to be found in David C. Douglas, *William the Conqueror* (London, 1964), and L. H. Nelson, *The Normans in South Wales* (London, 1966). Two other books appeared after this volume had been written: R. H. C. Davis, *The Normans and their Myth* (London, 1976), and D. C. Douglas, *The Norman Fate, 1100-1154* (London, 1976).

The Agrarian History of England and Wales, I, pt. ii, *A.D. 43-1042,* edited by H. P. R. Finberg (Cambridge, 1972). This contains an important essay by G. R. J. Jones on 'Post-Roman Wales'.

Barlow, F., *Edward the Confessor* (London, 1970).

Barrow, G. W. S., *Feudal Britain: the Completion of the Medieval Kingdoms, 1066-1314* (London, 1956).

Douglas, David C., *William the Conqueror* (London, 1964); *The Norman*

Achievement (London, 1969).

Ellis, T. P., *Welsh Tribal Law and Custom in the Middle Ages* (2 vols., Oxford, 1926).

Glamorgan County History, Vol. III, *The Middle Ages*, ed. T. B. Pugh (Cardiff, 1972).

Haskins, C. H., *The Normans in European History* (New York, 1915, with subsequent reprints).

Jones, Owain, and Walker, David, *Links with the Past: Swansea and Brecon Historical Essays* (Llandybie, 1974). This includes essays on 'Brecon Priory' and 'Gerald of Wales'.

Jones, Theophilus, *A History of the County of Brecknock* (Glanusk edition, 1898).

Lloyd, Sir John E., *A History of Carmarthenshire* (2 vols., Cardiff, 1935, 1939); *The Story of Ceredigion (400-1282)* (Cardiff, 1937); *A History of Wales from the Earliest Times to the Edwardian Conquest* (2 vols., 3rd. ed., London, 1948).

Millward, R. and Robinson, A., *The Welsh Marches, Landscapes of Britain* (London, 1971).

A Hundred Years of Welsh Archaeology, edited by V. E. Nash-Williams (Gloucester, 1946).

Nelson, L. H., *The Normans in South Wales, 1070-1171* (Austin, U.S.A., and London, 1966).

Pierce, T. Jones, *Medieval Welsh Society, Collected Papers*, ed. J. Beverley Smith (Cardiff, 1972).

Poole, A. L., *From Domesday Book to Magna Carta*, (2nd. ed., Oxford, 1955).

Rees, W., *South Wales and the March, 1284-1415* (Oxford, 1924, reprint 1974); *An Historical Atlas of Wales from Early to Modern Times* (Cardiff, new ed., 1959).

Renn, D. F., *Norman Castles* (2nd. ed., London, 1973).

Richter, M., *Giraldus Cambrensis* (Aberystwyth, 1973).

Rodd, Lord Rennell of, *Valley on the March* (Oxford, 1952).

Round, J. H., 'Introduction to the Worcestershire Domesday', *Victoria County History, Worcester*, vol. i, ed. H. A. Doubleday (London, 1901); 'Introduction to the Hereford Domesday', *Victoria County History, Hereford*, vol. i, ed. W. Page (London, 1908).

Stenton. F. M.. *Anglo-Saxon England* (3rd. ed., Oxford, 1970).

Sylvester, Dorothy, *The Rural Landscape of the Welsh Borderland* (London, 1969).

Tait, J., 'Introduction to the Shropshire Domesday', *Victoria County History, Shropshire*, vol. i, ed. W. Page (London, 1908).

Walker, David, *William the Conqueror* (Oxford, 1968).

Wightman, W. E., *The Lacy Family in England and Normandy, 1066-1194* (Oxford, 1968).

Warren, W. L., *King John* (London, 1961); *Henry II* (London, 1973)

Williams, A. H., *An Introduction to the History of Wales*, vol. ii, pt. i (Cardiff, 1939); *The History of Denbighshire* (Cardiff, 1950).

Of many articles and contributions to the work of learned societies, the following selection may be especially useful.

Edwards, J. G., 'The Normans and the Welsh March', *Proceedings of the British Academy, XLII* (1956).

Hogg, A. H. A., and King, D. J. Cathcart, 'Early Castles in Wales and the Marches: a preliminary list', *Archaeologia Cambrensis,* vol. 112 (1963).

King, D. J. Cathcart, 'The Castles of Breconshire', *Brycheiniog,* vol. 7 (1961).

King, D. J. Cathcart, and Spurgeon, C. J., 'The Mottes of the Vale of Montgomery', *Archaeologia Cambrensis,* vol. 114 (1965).

Lloyd, J. E., 'Wales and the Coming of the Normans (1039-1093)', *Transactions of the Honourable Society of Cymmrodorion,* 1899-1900.

Owen, H., 'The Flemings in Pembrokeshire', *Archaeologia Cambrensis,* 5th. series, vol. 12 (1895).

Index

Ewyas Harold, lordship of, 24, 31.
  priory of, 84.
Ewyas Lacy, lordship of, 25.
Exeter, 18.

Fforest Fawr, Brecknock, 35, 54.
Flanders, Bavanchore near Cassel,
  20, 21.
Flemings, in Ceredigion, 45, 46.
  in Pembrokeshire, 45.
  fostering in Welsh families, 75, 76, 80.
Framlingham, castle of, 61.
Fulford, battle of, 9.

Geoffrey ap Seisyll, 72.
Geoffrey, count of Brittany, 73.
Geoffrey Malaterra, 97.
Geoffrey de Mandeville, earl of Essex
  and Gloucester, 48.
Geoffrey of Neufmarché, 34.
Gerald of Wales, 46, 47, 56, 58, 62, 74,
  75, 78-81, 87, 90-93, 96, 97.
Gerald of Windsor,' 30, 41-43, 45, 62,
  63, 69, 74.
Gherbod, earl of Chester, 20.
Gilbert fitz Gilbert, of Clare, earl of
  Pembroke, 49.
Gilbert fitz Richard, of Clare, 45, 46,
  49.
Gilbert fitz Richard, earl of Hert-
  ford, 47.
Glamorgan (or Morgannwg), lord-
  ship of, 24, 37, 39, 40, 48, 65, 66, 78,
  85, 86, 88.
  shire-fee of, 40.
Glasbury, 34, 91.
Glasgrug, 46.
Gloucester, 15, 69.
  earldom of, 48.
  honour of, 37, 39, 48, 65.
  St. Peter's, abbey of, 39, 71, 84, 85.
Gloucestershire, 14, 21, 25, 52, 70, 71,
  77.
Glyn Rhondda, 39.
Godfrey, bishop of St. Asaph, 93.
Gower, lordship of, 42-45, 60.
Granville, family of, 40.
Gruffydd ab Idnerth ap Cadwgan, 36.
Gruffydd ap Cadwgan, 69, 75.

Gruffydd ap Cynan, prince of
  Gwynedd, 16, 27, 28, 30, 68, 75, 92.
Gruffydd ap Llywelyn, prince of
  Gwynedd, 13-16, 18, 65.
Gruffydd ap Maredudd ap Bleddyn,
  63.
Gruffydd ap Rhydderch, prince of
  Deheubarth, 13, 14.
Gruffydd ap Rhys, 46, 69, 96.
gwely, 54.
Gwenllian, daughter of Gruffydd ap
  Cynan, 75.
Gwent, 24, 58, 62, 73, 86, 88, 89.
Gwent, Nether, lordship of, 49.
gwestfa, 51.
Gwgan ap Meurig, 44.
Gwion, bishop of Bangor, 93.
Gwladus, wife of Seisyll ap Dyfnwal,
  72.
Gwynedd, 13, 15, 16, 29, 30, 50, 92.
Gwynllŵg, 16, 25, 39, 49, 85, 86, 89.
hafod, 52.
Harold of Ewyas, 31, 84.
Harold Godwineson, earl of Wessex,
  king of England, 9, 15, 18.
Hastings (or Senlac), battle of, 9, 10.
  Norman base at, 18, 56.
Hay, lordship of, 34, 35.
Hen Domen. See Montgomery.
Henry I, 22, 27, 39-45, 47, 49, 56,
  63, 70, 71, 77, 88, 96.
Henry II, 48, 61, 71, 73, 75, 77, 93.
Henry III, 58, 60, 70.
Henry ap Cadwgan, 69, 75.
Henry of Hereford, 71, 72.
Henry of Newburgh, earl of War-
  wick, 45.
Herbert fitz Herbert, 72.
Hereford, 14, 21, 23, 24, 67.
  bishop of, 87.
  earldom of, 20-22, 25, 27, 31, 71.
  St. Guthlac's, priory of, 84.
Herefordshire, 14, 21, 25, 34, 70, 71,
  79, 89.
Herewald, bishop of Llandaff, 88.
Hervé, bishop of Bangor, bishop of
  Ely, 87, 88.
Hubert de Burgh, 60, 77.
Hubert Walter, archbishop of
  Canterbury, 91.

Hugh of Avranches, earl of Chester, 20, 23, 27, 29, 30, 84.
Hugh, earl of Shrewsbury, 30, 42.
Humphrey de Bohun, 72.
Humphrey's Castle. *See Castell Hywel.*
Hywel ab Edwin, prince of Deheubarth, 13, 16.
Hywel ap Goronwy, 43, 44.
Hywel Dda, prince of Deheubarth, 13.

Iâl, lordship of, 26, 63.
Idnerth ap Cadwgan, 36.
Ifor ab Idnerth ap Cadwgan, 36.
Ifor Bach, lord of Senghennydd, 63.
Innocent III, pope, 91.
Iorwerth ap Bleddyn, prince of Powys, 40-43.
Iorwerth, brother of Morgan of Caerleon, 47.
Ireland, 51, 79, 90.
Norman invasion of, 10, 74, 75.
Irish, alliance with, 42.
Isabel, wife of King John, 48.
Is-Coed (Cards.), 46.
Italy, duchy of Calabria, 33.
Ithel, Domesday tenant, 52.

Joan, wife of Llywelyn the Great, 69, 70.
Is-Coed (Mon.), 24.
John, king, 48, 61, 69, 72-75, 77, 79.
Joseph, bishop of Llandaff, 89.

Kidwelly, castle of, 61, 64.
lordship of, 42-44.
priory of, 86.

Lacy, family of, 25, 31, 70, 84.
Lanfranc, archbishop of Canterbury, 85, 89.
Leinster, king of, 74.
Leofgar, bishop of Hereford, 14.
Lincoln, 75.
Lire, abbey of, 83.
Llanbadarn, 46.
Llancarfan, *clas* church of, 88.
Llandaff, diocese of, 87-90.
Llandaff, Book of, 88-90.

Llandovery, 36.
Llandybïe, 51.
Llanelwy. *See St. Asaph.*
Llangors, 73.
Llanrhystud, 47, 63.
Llanspyddid, 35.
Llowes, 91.
Llŷn peninsula, 29.
Llys Edwin, 58.
Llywel, 36.
Llywelyn ab Iorwerth, prince of Gwynedd, 11, 69, 70, 93.
Llywelyn ap Gruffydd, 69.
London, 18.
Tower of, 61.
London, family of, 85.
Lucy, wife of Herbert fitz Herbert, 72.
Ludlow, castle of, 24, 61.

Mabel of Bellême, wife of Roger of Montgomery, 22, 33.
Machen, 54.
Madog ap Cadwgan, 75.
Madog ap Maredudd, 63.
Maelgwyn ap Rhys, 64.
maenol, maenor, 50-52.
Maenol Bangor, 51.
Maenor Meddyfynych, 50, 51.
Magnus, king of Norway, 43.
Maihel of Hereford, 71.
Malpas, lord of, 27, 31.
Man, Isle of, 43.
Manorbier, castle of, 43, 62, 74.
marcher lords, powers of, 76-78.
Maredudd ab Owain, prince of Deheubarth, 24, 25.
Maredudd ab Owain ab Edwin, 16.
Maredudd ap Bleddyn, 41-43.
Maredudd ap Cadwgan, 75.
Margam, abbey of, 94.
Margaret de Bohun, 72.
Matilda, wife of William I, 22, 37.
Matilda the empress, queen of England, 71.
Maud, wife of Gruffydd ap Rhys, 69.
Maud of St. Valery, wife of William de Braiose, 73, 74.
Maurice of London, 45, 84.
Meisgyn, 39.
Mersete, hundred of, 25.

107

William II, 37, 77.
William of Barry, 74.
William of Brabant, 45.
William de Braiose, 69, 70, 72.
William de Braiose, 72-74, 77.
William, earl of Gloucester, 48, 63, 66, 84.
  daughters of, 48.
William fitz Baldwin, 44.
William fitz Osbern, earl of Hereford, 20-25, 31, 40, 83, 85.
William of London, 84.
William Marshal, earl of Pembroke, 49, 77.
William Pantulf, 33.
William Revel, 36.
Worcester, 61.
Worcestershire, 21.

York, 18, 21.
  Ystrad Meurig, castle of, 46, 47, 63.
Ystrad Peithyll, 46.
Ystrad Tywi, 42-44.
Ystradyw, 36.